Breathing
Life, A Mere Memoir

K.D.Brown

ROYSTON
Publishing

BK Royston Publishing
P. O. Box 4321
Jeffersonville, IN 47131
502-802-5385
http://www.bkroystonpublishing.com
bkroystonpublishing@gmail.com

© Copyright – 2022

All Rights Reserved. No part of this book may be reproduced, stored in a retrieval system, or transmitted by any means without the written permission of the author.

Cover Design: Elite Cover Designs
Cover Photos: K.D.Brown

ISBN-13: 978-1-955063-71-5

King James Version (KJV) - Public Domain

New King James Version (NKJV) - Scripture taken from the New King James Version®. Copyright © 1982 by Thomas Nelson. Used by permission. All rights reserved.

New International Version (NIV) - Holy Bible, New International Version®, NIV® Copyright ©1973, 1978, 1984, 2011 by Biblica, Inc.® Used by permission. All rights reserved worldwide.

Printed in the United States of America

So, what happened to the child
who was forced to grow up
wrapped in so many layers
of hurt and pain?
Did comfort
or love
come easy
and with no cost
or did the doors to more
hurt and pain open up once again?

I am so glad you asked…

Breathing

Life, A Mere Memoir

I dedicate this book to someone I am blessed and honored to call my husband and my peace. Garry McArthur Brown, I love you EVER so much.

You are one of the kindest, most supportive, humble persons I know who strives daily to make me happy, comfortable, and smiling, especially during my toughest moments. You stepped in and loved my three sons as your own and by far the BEST Buddy to our grandchildren. One thing I truly adore is how you know what to say (and not) when I am at my lowest. When I look across the room and see you knelt down praying at the side of the bed, I am reminded just how much you not only love me but continue to trust and love God as we journey through this thing, I call life. I could write another book full of hearts, memories, and thoughts of you but that is never needed as our bond from within continues to outward for all to see as our love story unfolds each day.

Blessed is the man who trusts in the Lord. Jeremiah 17:7 NIV

Acknowledgments

Always given to God the Father for without Him I would not be physically, emotionally, or mentally sound. During the darkest points in my life, when I thought I was forgotten and felt so broken, neglected, and abused, I now know He kept me. My Father, I love and praise you always.

My Babies, all of you! and those of you who the Lord continues allowing in my life, the glow of light you bring around me when I feel darkness approaching, brings so much comfort. Many blessings to you all, I know my life has been touched because our paths have crossed.

Special acknowledgments with so much love I will always send to my Auntie-Mommy Ernestine "Tina" Johnson, who through her own story of life continues to support and love me through my writings, while allowing me to seek names, dates, information, and truth from her always. Thank you so much my dearest auntie; I appreciate you so much.

Author's Note

I will continue to write about my journey as each letter, word, and page not only took forever to do, but also keep me whole within, as my mind revisits, regroups, and rebound, day in and day out as I also heal a pinch more each day. Healing not only comes from the joyous times, but in fact more from the moments that cause us broken, heart-wrenching pain which at times may stop our thoughts and reminds us to breathe. May we all continue to take one breath at a time.

Writing my life's experiences is never to cast blame or fault on another. It is merely to help uplift myself as I make some sense of what I had to endure while having hopes that sharing a piece of my journey will help another as they read my story. To all whom the Lord guides to read any of my writings, I pray that you take my words and allow them to minister within, break the chapters apart, highlight words, sentences or paragraphs that stand out or hit close to home, then write notes next to what moved, touched, or gave you some peace at that moment. For if my story can comfort and start the healing process for one, then my mission in this thing I call life will have been met.

Prologue

As more memories surface from my past the urge to keep sharing rises.

As past trauma lingers while new hurt and pain knock at the door, the urge to share heightens.

As the nerves and trembles take over from time to time, I remember to take longer breaths, while thinking of a childhood which was stripped from me so painfully, my child who was taken from me so abruptly and hope which was almost taken forever.

As I pause to sadly reminisce over my past, I grab a hold of the little pieces of love, kindness, and portrayal of what I created to fill the gap of what I thought was normal life and tell me it could have been worse.

As I continue to look up daily for more comforting memories, a true smile from within and more pieces to the puzzle of understanding my life, I think of Proverbs 19:8 *"Whoever gets sense loves his own soul; he who keeps understanding will discover good."* (ESV)

As I ponder that scripture, I silently repeat it to myself several times, close my eyes, then whisper it softly several times while allowing the 14-word scripture minister to me as if it were 14 thousand words.

I continue to be amazed by my sense, soul, understanding, and good I have deep within.

Daily I realize that one purpose in my life is to write, share, and continue to love hard, in spite of it all. Thoughts and questions linger in my mind periodically, as I continue to piece it all together. The little girl in me can breathe a little lighter as her breath stops fluttering and she courageously whispers, "I made it one breath at a time."

As hard as it is to continue to write and share a story, my story in which I am still living, I know I must if not for me, for another who is or may have lived one chapter along with me. Sometimes you have to get up and appear to be great! Put on some hope and allow grace in while showing mercy toward others, especially during your toughest days. I know this is easier said than done and may even look great on paper. As I gaze out the window gathering my thoughts while wanting to share it all with you and be as raw as I can, I ask you to pull back while reading, push judgment and assumptions aside, and fall so far into my journey so that when you finish letting my words slowly roll off your lips, someone who may need to hear them can, as at that moment healing for another may manifest. Strength from within can abound and tears that stayed so far within can flow.

My wish is not to write because it is great to pass the time, but to inspire one person to know just how important you are!

Let us

Stay Inspired

Keep Believing

Sharing & Doing

Someone Needs

A Push From

Your Story

My Loves,

The overwhelming feeling, I get each time I think of each and every one of you, because of you all I stay whole. To my sons Daryl, Eddie, Douglas, and granddaughters McKenzie, Kamryn, Penelope, and Kyree; when you look as far as your eyes can see, know that is how much I adore you.

"Lo, children *are* an heritage of the LORD: *and* the fruit of the womb *is his* reward."
Psalms 127:3 KJV

This Christmas. Forever 2017'

* * * * * * * * * * * * * * *

Growing up with so much freedom but no freedom within was interesting as I look back now and realize that I never fully knew who I was or can remember having an identity that I could relate to. Hmmm. I guess I can pat myself on the back for keeping my composure more than less through it all, while looking above to whisper, "Thank You Lord…for keeping me whole, together, and sane through it all." After enduring more than I have seen in hundreds of movies during the early years of my life, I could only think life would have to get easier if only for a period. I continue to go through past periods in my mind that are a blur, as at times remembering would prove traumatic! I allow grace and mercy to gently bring memories back when they are supposed to come. Am I angry, upset or hurt by my life? I would say yes and no. "Yes," because I was stripped from being able to be a child while enjoying childhood as a child should; "yes," because I miss and long for a mother I will never know; "yes," because I — like many others — still deal with the trauma and triggers of it all; and "yes," because it continues to take the rest of my life to learn who Karen is. I would in turn say "no," because deep in my heart I believe what I endured was merely training for the grown-up person I was to become; "no," because it made the scared, weak, and lost child so much stronger; and "no," because her in mind in spite of it all she remembered how to smile. How did I go on as if behind the front door of the cute four-bedroom brown house with the nice hedges along the property line and manicured neighborhood was a happy place without fault? How did I push forward after being bullied on the outside, while being touched as a child should never be on the inside, just how when an eating disorder had taken over? How simple was it, I worked harder than I thought I could, smiled when wanting to cry and kept moving forward while forcing the past as far behind me as I thought I could?

How many people know it's not as easy to walk away from a past that would always be so close behind, arise with a smell, thought or glimpse of what used to be? To now know that triggers (anything that remind someone of past trauma/hurt) will always be a part of my life causes me to work daily at understanding as well as how to cope and deal overall. Never will this be easy, but with my best friends Grace and Mercy, I shall push, run, and many days keep crawling so not to be in the dark places of my past, if even in my head.

As I reflect on some things, I spoke of in my first book while remembering my younger self, I sadly remember so much pain within, never having an outlet to release while reminding my little self, no matter what you do keep breathing. I thank God each day that He kept His hands on me back then and more today. So, the girl named Karen could learn to have life after losing her mother who was murdered when she was six years old, having been molested by an uncle and a stepbrother, being bullied in grade school by the girl whose face and acts she could still see today along with other kids who thought the acts were funny, losing a brother to suicide, and dealing with an eating disorder because of the word we now know as Trauma, as she understands now that trouble may not last always, but trials and tribulations do continue to come and go.

We are stronger than we will ever know, but sadly many of us won't realize this until so much later.

> *He gives strength to the weary and increases the power of the weak.*
> Isaiah 40:29 (NIV)

How was I supposed to ever know what a healthy relationship was? I surely could not go by what was displayed around me as I was touched inappropriately by people and was so confused, or was I confused at that time, as are any victims, especially children, confused since it is all we knew. Did we think this was normal? Was this happening in all houses? I am sure that crosses many minds as it did mine as a child. So how would dating look like to a child who was introduced to the physical while not yet having understanding of a healthy mental or emotional relationship? In my case, she would date the wrong people.

Would you call it dating? What really made hook-ups back in the 80's while in middle school or high school "official"? My goodness, as I think about it why did I think some of my grown-up relationships were official? I strayed into unhealthy relationships and situations not necessarily because I wanted to, but because I could. Lack of parental guidance, structure, along with sexual acts being performed on you as a child = No One Cares About You Anyway! Plus, in my little mind it was what was expected. I share this to heighten awareness, for someone who feels something is wrong within the home, within themselves, or for another. It is time to act upon the instincts, step out on faith, and do something about it. Parents: pay attention the right way, not by loving through gifts and too much freedom. You will be surprised not only how much your children need positive discipline, chores, and healthy responsibilities, while you coach, mentor, and love them more than anyone else. For the world within the home is supposed to be the comfort zone with so much trust and not another place in which a child is scared to dwell.

Can we stop quoting "our children are the future" at the same time that we expect them to not acknowledge or learn from the present or past? When we think the questions we may have wanted to ask of a parent or guardian, although time, circumstance, or lack of any communication stopped us, we end up with more unanswered questions added to the list of the unknowns. Think of the ones you may have or had, then the ones you know your child may be thinking of asking but something is holding them back.

I answered these to young Karen who still wondered, while she remembers all she has ever poured into her own children.

Who am I?
You are everything and so much more
What am I?
Exactly what you were created to be
Why am I?
You were created to be a bridge for so many, just like your mother
Where am I?
Where you're supposed to be, even when uncomfortable, tired, and want to give up, remember keep the faith; a change is coming. You are doing great!
Will I?
Yes, you will do everything
Can I?
Oh, you can achieve and do it all, remember what you have accomplished already, your family is so proud of you
Is my body mine?
Yes precious, your body is your temple created by God, it is for you to know far before anyone else
Am I special?
More than you will ever know
And And And

Take a moment and ask yourself these questions, then should you have children, discuss their questions while allowing them to freely talk with no judgment or facial expressions from you. Be kind and allow them to express and be themselves always!

You will be amazed how one small conversation can create, rebuild, or enhance your relationships, while encouraging another to love and understand self-worth.

I am thankful that I always knew deep within the life I was tossed into as a child, was merely what I still call training for what my future held. For a long time, I knew I was in a bad dream and would awake to what some call a normal life. Sadly, it was not until I was a late teen that reality struck; I was awakened, and I finally realized that these were the cards I had been dealt to play.

I would then stop longing for the dad who I remembered playing music, the sound of his laughter, how I could tell when it was good laughter or not. I always dreamed and then hoped he would walk me down the aisle at my wedding, as I thought of that special moment, if only for a moment. While internally also embracing a granddad who would spend time with my children, this, too, was a mere thought and still unbelievably a reality. Fairytales and television lifestyles are just that: a written story that looks great on the outside, with extravagant colors, smiles gleaming, and of course the family dynamic with every piece and person intact. My new normal was to remind myself not to set expectations so high for another while doing what I had been programmed all my life to do: regroup, pull together whatever I had left within me, and make something happen while smiling through it all, while carrying my mother's passion and drive, which I know continues to run gracefully through me. Oh, to hear and remember her voice just one more time, receive a tight hug, get some advice, and watch her embrace my babies. What many take for granted others such as me miss terribly. My goodness, where do I go from here?

Growing up, we attended church at times, which did nothing for the situations occurring within the household, relationships with family members or even God at the time.

Sure, my stepmother's church, St. John's Episcopal, accepted us children; we sang in the choir (and Mr. Russell the choir director/organist was very nice) received our first communion, enjoyed summer camps and all, but why were we there? Who was God? Who were these people who looked nothing like us and acted so different?

Having been born Baptist, with my mother singing within the choir, causes me to add another what if and how would my life had been if we continued fellowship in the Baptist church, her church with her memories. With someone saying, "sing this song like your mother," viewing a possible photo of her in the church dining hall, and feeling her presence as pieces of her faith and love embraced us just one more time. Being within the Baptist church now, I absorb pieces of everyone's history, take in the stories down to the last key played from the hymnals, while grasping on to the ways of the church mothers as the child in me whispers, "I know my mommy was like this" or would have been like that. Oh, how much is taken when someone is taken.

Situations as such take my mind into a deeper place as I continue to wonder who is supposed to sit the children down and say this is why…this is because…. This will always ring through my thoughts, especially since my mother was taken so abruptly, followed by "hello, nice to meet you" from an unknown world.

Will I ever piece together the puzzle, timelines, addresses, dates, who or why? Possibly not. Sadly, the one who can close up some gaps for me, will not and may carry to the grave so many of the answers that can ease my mind, spirit, and heart. Having learned late in life (year 2020, 45 years after my mother's passing) from a cousin that shortly after my mother was murdered, she and some other cousins were sat down, and explained that we (Pat's children) were to be treated different (special, better, I guess) from then on out, since our mother was taken. She also said we were never to be told of the conversation that was held. This was another "wow factor" in my life as I continue to wonder if it's all a dream and, one day, I will wake to whatever a normal life was to be.

When will we get to the point that we stop hiding the truths of it all so the pain could stop and not linger for 44, 64, or 84 years? Why must we continue guessing and wondering? Why do we have children holding unexplained secrets just because we think it is helping the situation? Can't we see we're only causing more stress on the children who are suffering and also on the children who must keep such secrets within? I'm sure some resentment toward Pat's special children had to present itself at one time or another. I no longer say generational curses, because when we do, we allow a negative past to overshadow the healing and growth that tries to come forward. How much different could my life had been had guilt, sorrow, and hurt not overcome so many who tried to protect me. I sadly say "tried," as trying was all one could do while trying to heal from a broken past also. Starting today, let's try and do better for those coming behind us. May we stop trying to hide hurtful pasts which will, in fact, reveal itself regardless of what we do or not.

What and why is a grandparent? I can't speak on behalf of anyone else except myself as I am now extremely blessed to be a grandparent ("Nona") and couldn't imagine my life without my babies and now grandbabies. Understanding trauma and relationships as I do now, I realize why some make their choices, although I also believe our children should never have to suffer because of another's actions or lack of. The time is now to pull a hold of ourselves, if not for ourselves then for the children who will one day sit wondering as they think of the smallest question with the largest impact: "Why?"

Having been that child who grew up wondering the why's within far too many aspects of my life, I strive to do better, be better, and show better. I know I love hard, and that I attribute to my mother, who loved the way she wished to have been loved.

Oh, to see her face as I'm sure she hurt deep within while watching me go through more than any parent would ever want a child to bare, only to shout "Hallelujah!" now as she watches and helps me rise higher each day! I sit smiling with a feeling within as I take a deep breath slowly while thinking of her and the grandmother she would have been to my babies and her great-grandchildren.

Striving to fill such a large void while always doing and thinking as I know she would have causes me to push more than I probably should at times, for if only a moment that keeps me full of her presence that fills me within, then I shall carry on as such.

Missing the presence of my own except for one grandmother during my life, I will continue being Nona for mine and so many others who I pray will not have to think so hard later in life while wondering how a grandparent's love should feel.

I thank God for the role my grandmother's partner, Mr. Milton (Rob) Robinson, played within my life as a child and young adult, for had it not been for him I would have never experienced a piece of a grandfather's love, wisdom, lessons, and the structure of what a grandfather should exhibit. I will keep the memories of growing up and visiting a home in which I felt love, peace, and joy after asking the bus driver repeatedly, "are we there yet" as the anticipation of arriving somewhere peaceful in my childhood placed me in a happy place. Prior to my grandmother moving to this home in Danbury, Connecticut, life was quite different at her apartments as in the vibe, feelings, constant movement with family coming and going, lots of talking, just busy. We lived with her and some aunts and uncles before my father came to retrieve us once settled in after my mother's death. Reflecting back to our Danbury time, I so enjoyed my grandmother and Mr. Rob picking us up from the bus stop in one of his old cars, the car was a model from the 30's or 40's. They were cool along with all the stories that came with the rides.

I also hold his sister, Aunt Greta, close to my heart. The smell of her home, the sweets she baked, and the big feeling of warmth I felt from such a small woman will always remind me that the Lord does fill voids when we don't realize it until so much later.

I have to be honest and say her treats did have a unique taste that you had to grow to appreciate, but nonetheless I do miss them both and the priceless legacy of two people who lived close to or a bit over 100 years of age. Having no photos with them doesn't matter as I can still see their faces as if it were yesterday. I am blessed to have and cherish a small dresser of Aunt Greta's, which I was told she used as a child, while remembering also how much my grandmother loved it when she would tell me stories about how she obtained it and her relationship with Aunt Greta. Closing my eyes, I can see the small dresser sitting in my grandmother's bedroom, a nightstand next to her white cast iron bed made up with a white blanket with the puffy cotton balls on it.

Mr. Rob and his sister didn't have to love or accept any of us, but am I so grateful that they did! I'm sure like many families some others may have felt and dealt different cards, but these are my memories for which I am grateful.

I don't know who needs to re-read this chapter for closure, acceptance or to say I need to be the bigger person, I need to be the best grandparent or grandparent figure starting today, for if I decide to be so, someone will not only have better memories to cherish later, but a better life today while becoming who they are to be sooner than later.

I am so blessed that the Lord saw fit to open the doors of Mr. Rob's home to my siblings and me if only for a moment. I thank the Lord for allowing a man to love us in the grandfather way, for a man who selflessly loved and shared his home, a man who contacted me when my grandmother passed (at that time they had since parted and she was residing in Virginia with me) and contacted me to see how I was doing and if I needed anything, a man who always kept a calm voice even when sharing some not-too-funny jokes. Knowing they had issues as all relationships do, I appreciate still today that the issues were never shared or shown amongst us children. Let me shout a really quick "hallelujah!" then whisper "Thank You, Lord" for providing an example of maturity that should always be held in front of children, so for a moment the children don't have to feel fear, for a moment they know what caring means, and for many moments to come they can apply the same maturity as life charges at them in all directions once an adult. Sadly, I will never be able to say any of this about my blood grandparents, but I also know that blood is not always what makes up a family.

My recommendation is that we continue or start reflecting on who is or has been sent into our lives to fill a void, instead of always crying over who is not a part of it.

When we feel love we become love — When we are love, we give love

Thinking, being, doing as you reflect on so much is extremely hard. The mind drifts to the child you thought you once were but in reality, still are. You remember who was and who wasn't and, my Lord, who you feel should have never been. Comparing what you cannot forget while trying harder than ever to erase memories from within as the horrid thought of ever having to relive so much hurt brings on instant stomachache and chills that take a moment to shake off, while reminding yourself to take a breath. At this moment, you tell yourself those seasons did teach you something. The pain of it all has strengthened you a little more and the memories remind you of what shall never be repeated.

Being human, we will always hold some regrets, but let us not carry another's as our own bags are heavy enough by themselves. Family, friends, associates, people in general will be who they are regardless of how you enter or exit their lives, having learned that no matter what, it is always best to "Stay True to You and Yours." In doing so, the season of certain people in your life will change accordingly and exactly when needed. May we stop seeking until we are drained having no energy, stop trying for what will never be and stop begging when the answers have already been answered long ago. Dream new dreams, make new traditions with whom and what you have, live each day to the fullest, smile even when crying of a past memory, heads up when others expect it to be low, be more to you than you ever thought you could be, and at the end of a trying day before you lay your head down, say "Lord, thank you for keeping and pushing me because it wasn't easy today." Then rest, knowing you did get the last word and spoke it to the right person.

The LORD is my shepherd; I shall not want. ²He maketh me to lie down in green pastures: he leadeth me beside the still waters. ³He restoreth my soul: he leadeth me in the paths of righteousness for his name's sake. ⁴Yea, though I walk through the valley of the shadow of death, I will fear no evil: for thou art with me; thy rod and thy staff they comfort me. ⁵Thou preparest a table before me in the presence of mine enemies: thou anointest my head with oil; my cup runneth over. ⁶Surely goodness and mercy shall follow me all the days of my life: and I will dwell in the house of the LORD forever. Amen.   Psalm 23 (KJV)

REMEMBERING

Mommy: Patricia Ella Dickson, Daddy: Coleridge John Dickson II
Lorrena (Lisa), Myself, Kathy (my Twin) and Andrew (Mit)
Our love and strong hope have always prevailed

Front: Aunt Victoria "Vicky", my Sister Lisa on our Great Grandmothers lap, Uncle Alan "Red" (my mother's youngest siblings) Standing: Grandma Lorena Johnson and my mother smiling that smile we still try to carry on today.

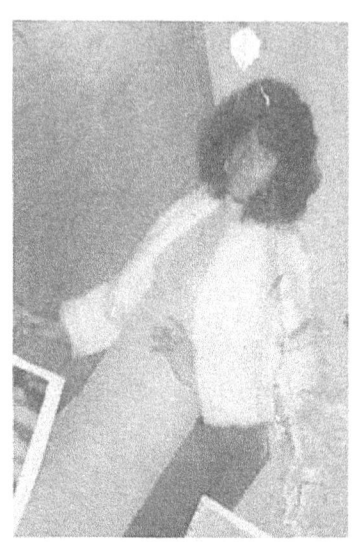

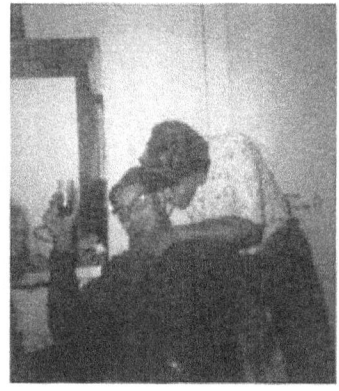

Front: Great Grandma Kathleen Crosley McKelvey holding Uncle Alan Uncle Charles, Great Aunt Elizabeth "Goo" McKelvy Minor "Goo", My Mom, Grandma Lorrena "Toots" McKelvy Johnson, Great Aunt Johnnie Mae McKelvy McCord "Mickie" (Grandma Sisters)

My Mother happy with Uncle Charles Minor He was married to my Grandma's sister my Great Aunt Goo.

PATRICIA ELLA JOHNSON

Mothers HS Graduation Class of 66'

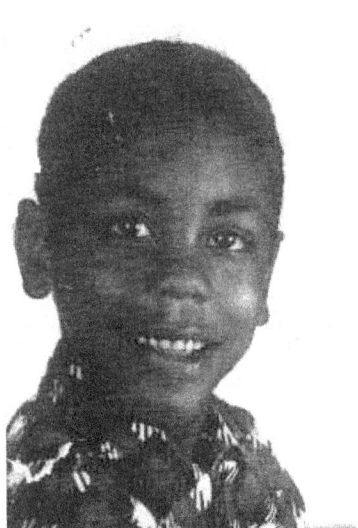

Father 2nd grade school picture
Yes, I always had his face!

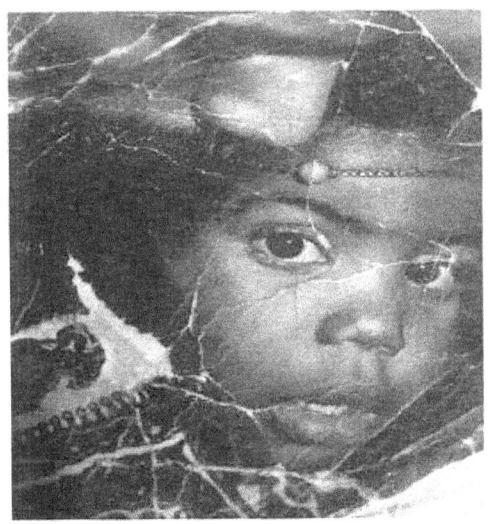

Dad and Myself
Black History Program, Stamford Connecticut 1971
I will always appreciate the music, culture, and strength learned from my daddy, even when he did not think I was paying attention to him trying.

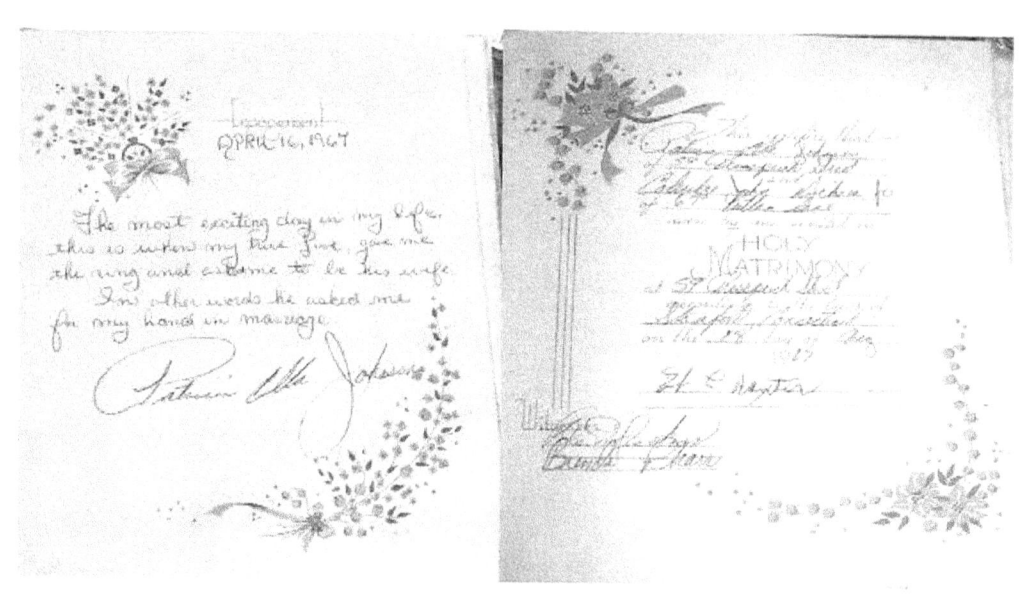

My Parents say *"I DO"* August 18, 1967

Mom, Aunt Denise (Dad Sister) Brenda Farr, and women on far right believed to be a lady my mother allowed to live with her along with her son.

Jerry McCullen, Johnny Jr., (Aunt Tina Fiancé'), Dad, unknown, Great Uncle Charles

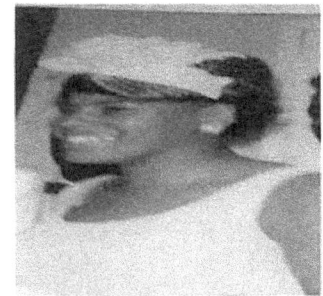

Paternal Great Grandmother Corine & Grandmother Dorothy Unknown (possibly Grandma Dorothy 2nd husband), Mom, Dad, Maternal Grandmother Lorrena

Grandmother Corine, Grandmother Lorrena, unknown, Aunt Denise (Dad Sister), Mom, Brenda (mom's best friend), Aunt Ernestine "Tina" (Mom Sister), Grandmother Dorothy and Great Aunt Micky (Grandma Lorrena Sister)

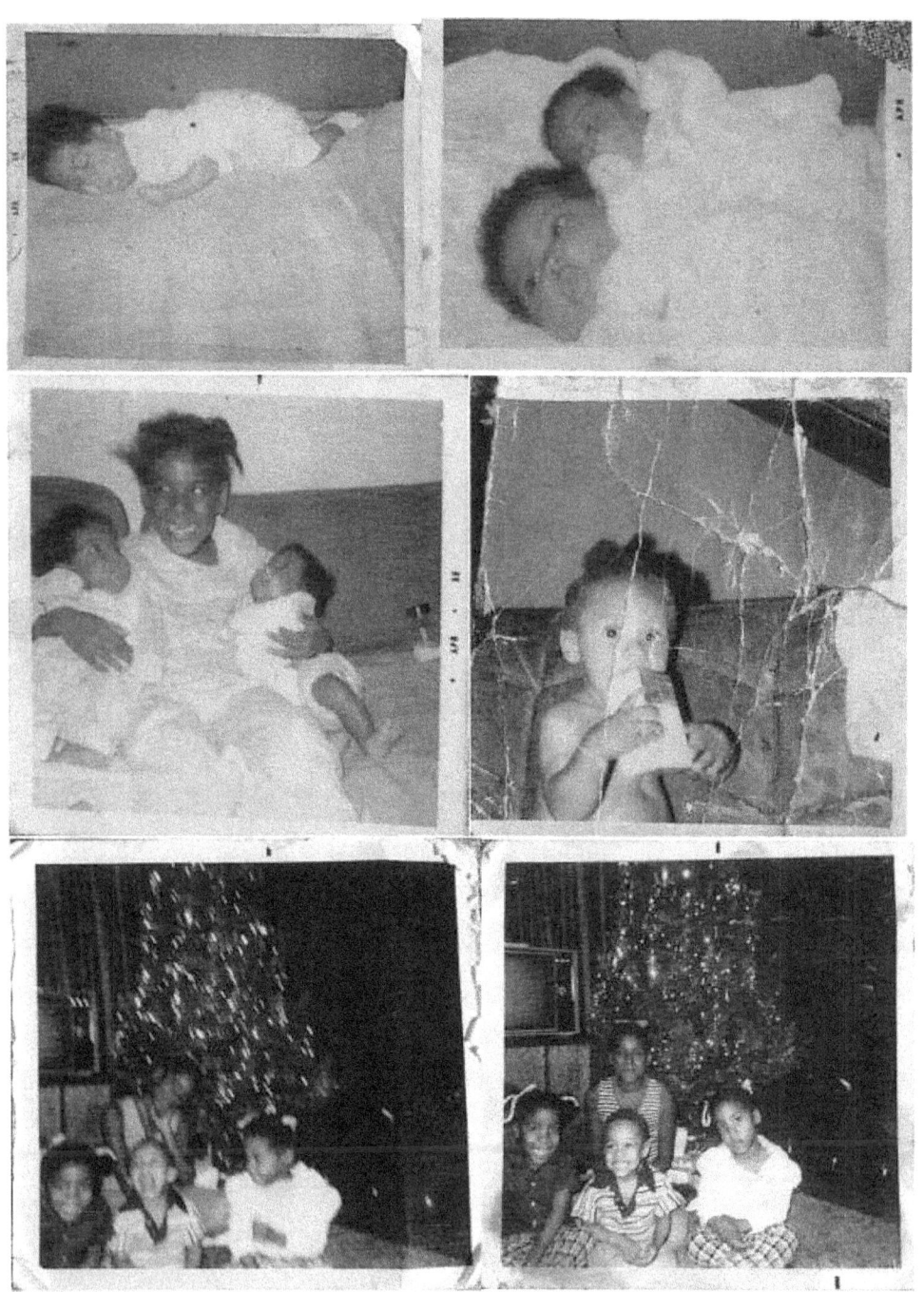

April 1969 our big sister enjoys the twins, she still loves us! I believe the picture of my brother (alone) is early 1971, he was always the cutest and most spoiled. Christmas (I believe 1974, last one with our mother) my brother who always started trouble NEVER got in trouble, can you guess who got in trouble for punching him after he was bothering me.

Kathy & Karen

Outside playing, photo with dads friends 1970's, My dad being silly with my brother and myself sometime around 1981. I still can hear his laugh in my mind which as it still makes me smile (ironically my husband's laugh reminds me of my dad), and as always some love from our Great Uncle Charles who was truly the NICEST person in the world! Christmas 1969.

School Pictures 1975 – 1978

I believe I only had one or two more taken after these, I would think why keep smiling over the pain, also for a period of time school became just as hard to cope with as home.

My brother Mit and I enjoying the water sprinkler in the backyard at our home on Moffitt St. in Connecticut (around 1980-81. To laugh and have natural fun as you forget it all for a moment. My sister and brother dancing as my father played music always, we so enjoyed that and having our own headphones hooked up to his stereo system. I can still see his wall to wall crates of albums, the bongo's, and conga he had as music was a true staple in the house. I believe that helped us through more than we knew.

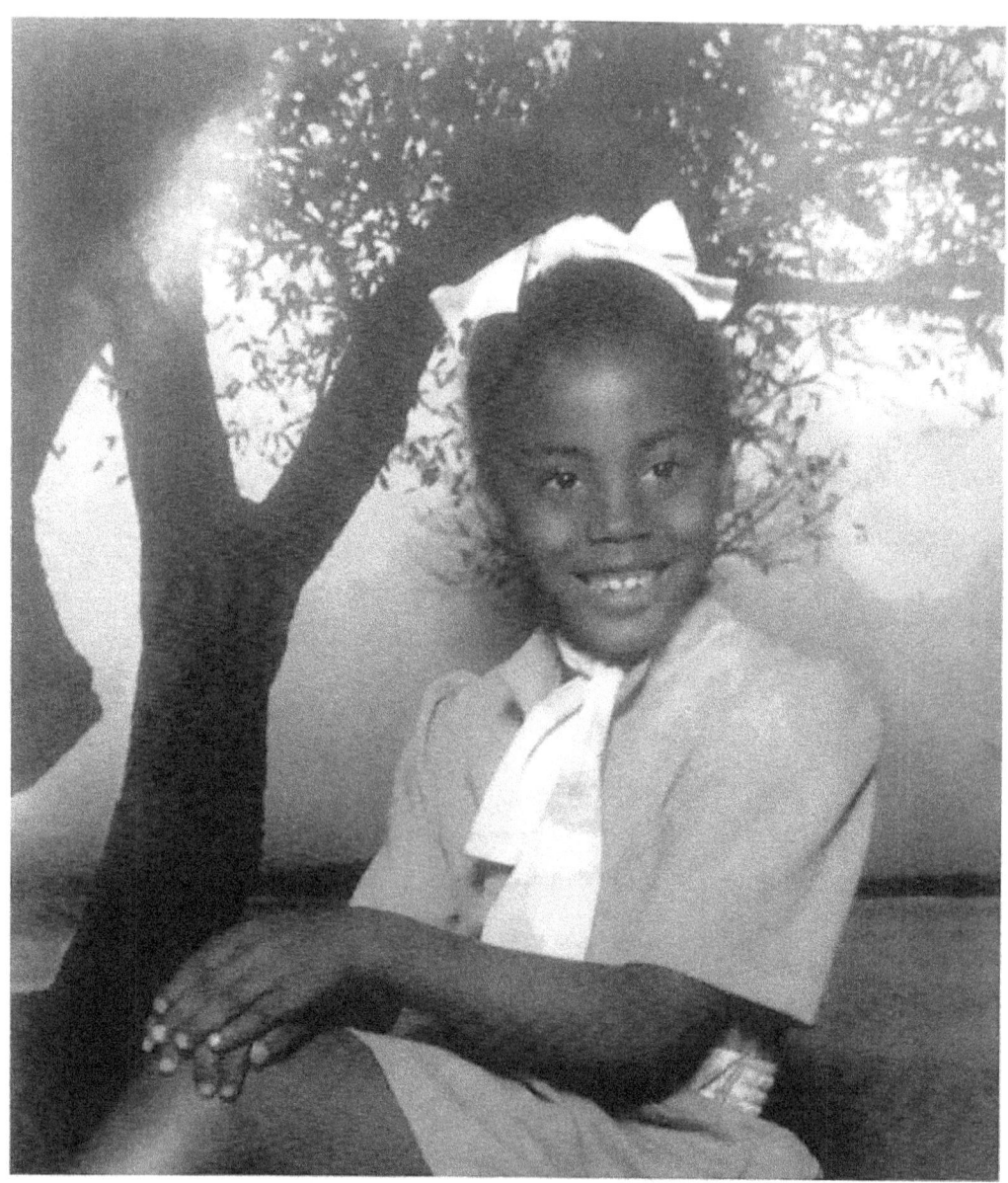

After losing a mother she still smiled, for understanding has yet to sink in. Photo taken after saving my money with Aunt Vicky who took me to take the picture around 1977. I learned later in life my mother's family made a bond to protect and treat "Pat's Kids" different, special, etc. they did their best while we were still with them. Shortly after moving from them while still not fully understanding where my mother had gone, and this new family my father moved us with, my world would drastically change once again.

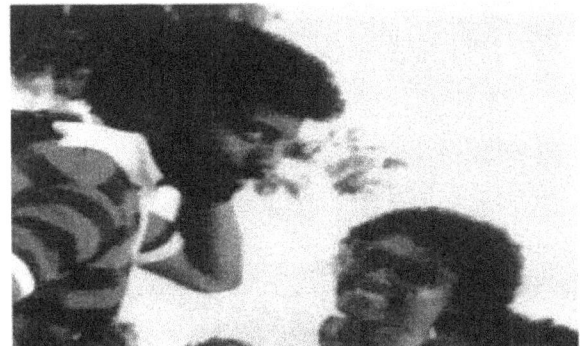

Dad with Suzanne Smith Dickson, married 1977 - Divorced 1987, the only woman I have called and still my stepmother, being the only one in my life during childhood. The others came after I was an adult.

Douglas Vincent Smith
(Suzanne's Son) my stepbrother who was an artist and ballet dancer. I always respected him because he respected me! He loved to play jokes on us, and tolerated us even though he was not happy about his small family becoming so large after our parents married. He will never know how much I admired him, his drive and for being smart enough to move away when opportunity arose. May he continue to watch over us and guide us when see fit. Always wanting to remember him, I named my last son Douglas. I had another step brother (Curtis) although no healthy bond to speak of nor share... My father and Suzanne also shared a beautiful daughter together my little sister "Kaliah" who also continues to love us from above.

Suzanne's church where we attended and took part in the children's choir, Sunday school, and received our first communion. St. John's Episcopal Church, Bridgeport Connecticut around 1978-79. My brother Andrew "Mit" school picture I believe to be 1984, and Myself, Kathy and Mit took a picture together at the mall, our older sister Lisa and two step brothers Douglas and Curtis were supposed to take part, we ran around all day looking for them "on a city bus" and well you see who made it. Photo believed to be between 1985-87.

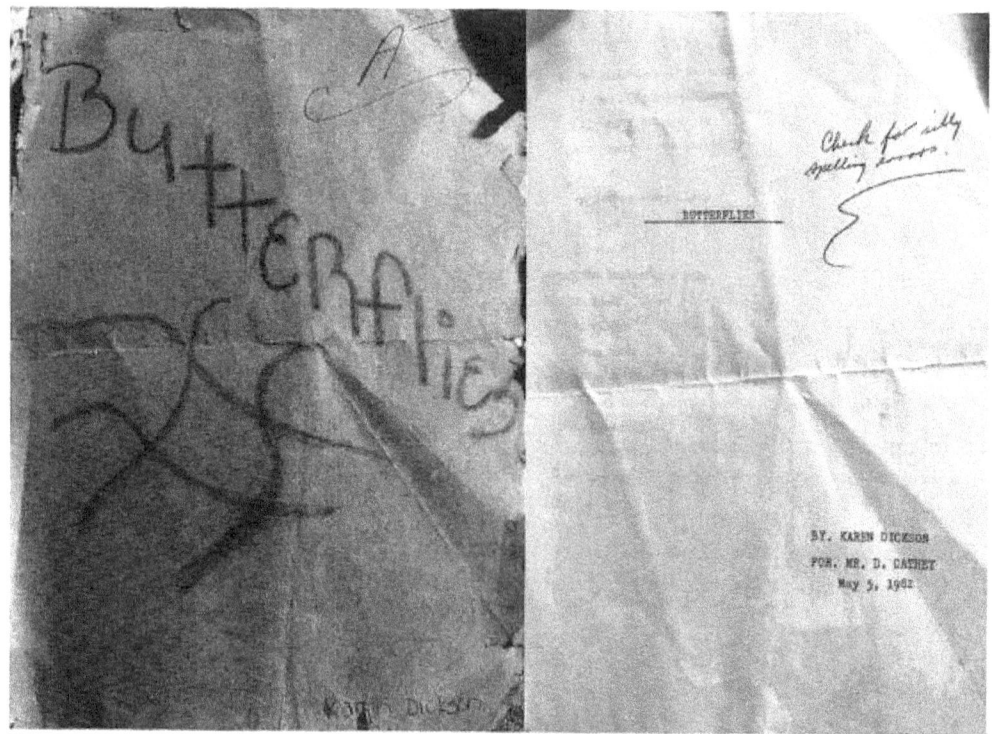

How ironic a book report that I wrote so long ago; May 5, 1982 and saved would be about Butterflies. Oh the significance of them back then and so much more to me now. Mr. Cathey was a wonderful teacher! I thank him for the A- and the constructive criticism "check for silly errors" ha ha I still have to!

Photo believed to be taken at sears around 1983, I went with friends to take although my so called boyfriend didn't show up, story of my life way back when... Make a note to self: always put you first and if you have to take a selfie instead of a picture, do just that!

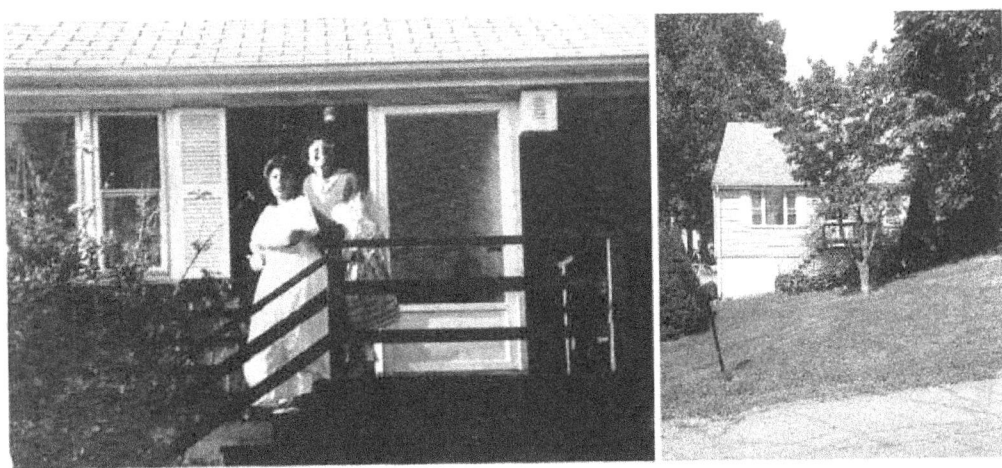

Suzanne, stepmom who was excited about my prom, always has the prettiest smile. 104 Moffitt Street, Bridgeport Connecticut 1986 "Senior Prom Day". Wow the house we lived in for about 10 years, the 4 bedroom, one bath home now looks so small although holds so many big memories. Look at the big alarm box, which was very LOUD, security sure has come a long way. I wonder who lives here today and if they have a happy home within. Photo on right of house taken 9/1/2020, how my heart fluttered to be parked in front of this house after so many years.

Prom 1986' Linda Mosley, Me, Leslie Mosley, And my sister Kathy "The Twins"

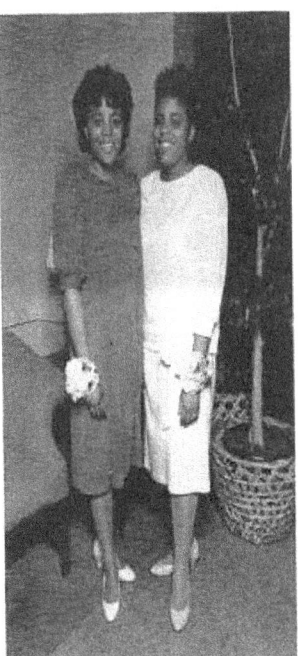

Junior Ring Dance 1985' "Kathy and Myself" I was sick with a cold although attended and received my Highschool class ring

Photo taken 1984 or 1985 during the annual rivalry Thanksgiving Day Football Game Central vs Harding. I was part of the Color Guard with Central High School & loved twirling the rifle, marching with the band and of course the competitions "Go Hilltoppers"

Hanging at the Mall 1985 with some of the girls outside of Dunkin Donuts where a few of us worked. Our nicknames were on our Santa hats. Pinky (me), Jiggy for Janet and Tinky for Tina.

WE, THE MEMBERS OF THE CLASS OF 1986

. . . . BEING OF SOUND AND GENEROUS MIND, AND FORESEEING OUR IMPENDING DEPARTURE FROM THE WORLD IN WHICH WE HAVE ENJOYED OUR ADOLESCENT YEARS, DO PUBLISH THIS, OUR LAST WILL AND TESTAMENT, AND DO JOINTLY AND SEVERALLY MAKE THE FOLLOWING BEQUESTS:

I, **Karen Yvette Dickson, (Pinky)**, hereby leave
- my "lil" brother Andrew Dickson "Mit" the ability to pass with his class and do less yelling around the halls.
- I leave Tina Marie Rhodes the ability to stop skipping so much and stop hanging around the wrong people so she will have some friends.
- I also leave my cousins Lawrence and Maurice Dickson the ability to do good and stop saying "I didn't say that," "I know" and "I didn't do that."
- I leave Kimberly Mosely the best of luck!
- I leave James Jones my locker, all to himself, since he acted like it was his anyway. I also leave him the ability to try and solve his problems with Tara Rogers.
- I leave the class of '87 the ability to party hard like we the class of '86 did. Good luck, '87. You're gonna need it!

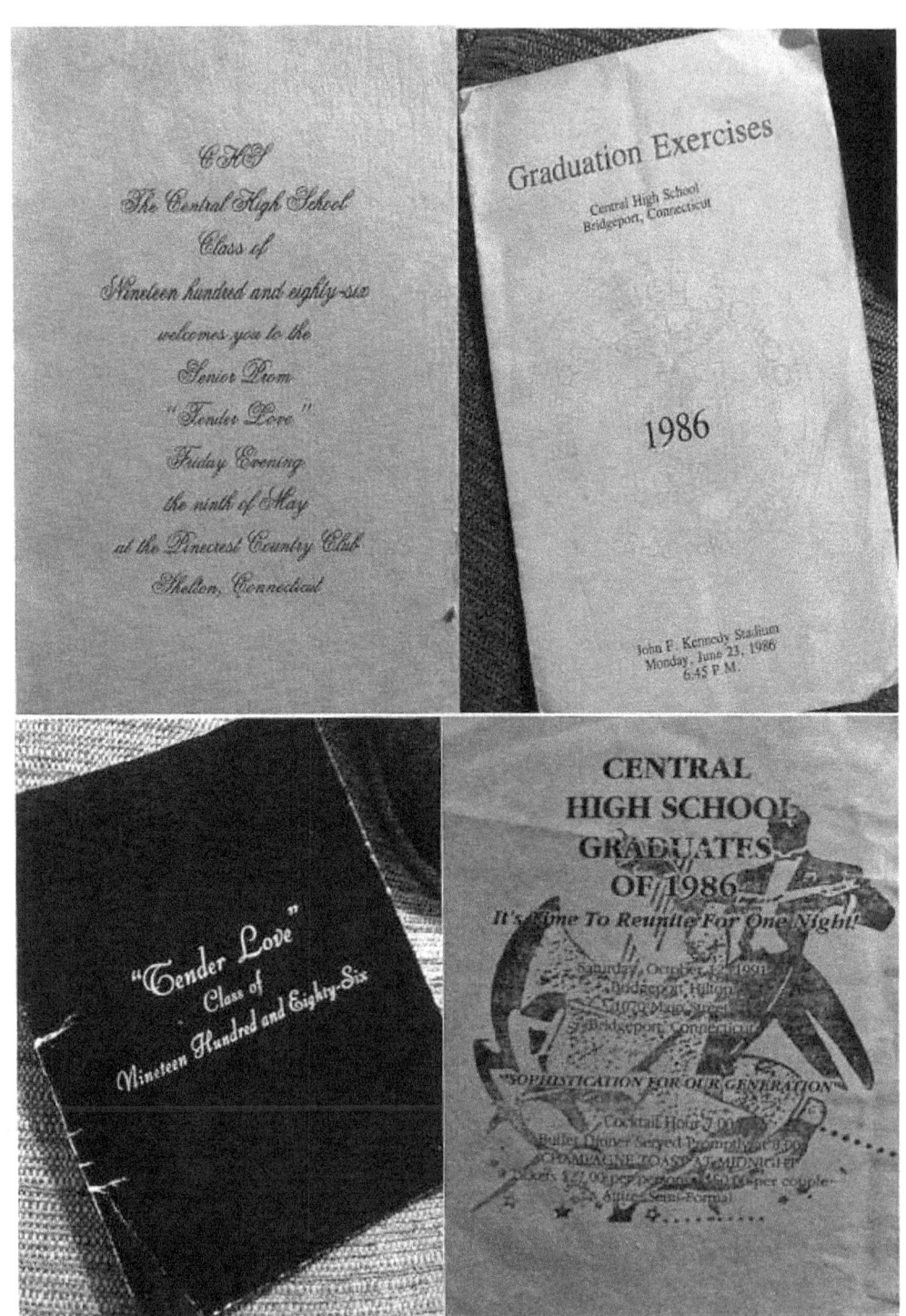

Having many aunts, uncles, and cousins as both sides of my family are exceptionally large. I share many memories with them all, some good and like many families some not, many of which I cherish since childhood as I have always carried a special bond whether near or far.

Uncle Darrell Dickson & Aunt Denise Dickson-Wells (my father's siblings) I have always looked up to you and adore how you adore and love all no matter how tough times got. Auntie thank you for taking this picture, well we made you! after not being together in 14 years. Love you both dearly. 2019

My Cousins Lawrence Dickson & Deidre Dickson-McNeil you will never know how much I appreciate & love our bond "more like siblings since day 1" even though Lawrence cares for us all like a parent! 2019 Aunt Denise Children.

My Auntie Mommy Ernestine "Tina" Johnson Words cannot describe our bond and love. I am forever grateful for emotionally filling my mother's shoes in her absence.

Uncle Dwane Dickson, my father's baby brother, always loved me as a uncle should have and still do. Since I was a child, he would say how wise I was, with a good head on my shoulders and he could see something special about me. Thank you for always telling me what all broken children need to hear. I love you so much! Like you, I will always seek answers from deep within about our family, one day we shall have closure and peace.

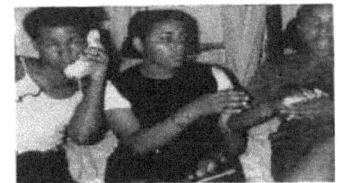

Tashina Johnson, Oh my little cousin/god sister. Aunt Linda Johnson daughter, the "Spoiled One" always had to sit in the middle and still says we are really triplets. Guess she is not in the middle in the picture above as the phone cord couldn't reach (early 1980's). "Tash" may you always exhibit the inner strength you have, which is beyond your years, true beautiful inside and out. I cherish our bond, love, and random talks!

My Auntie Mommy "Aunt Tina"
My mother continued through her so I could know a mothers love.

My Dear Grandmother Lorrena "Toots"
I will forever feel the love she had for my mother and myself.

Great Grandmother Corine so elegant and graceful, I will always cherish a pink crystal dish I received after her passing, while always wondering how our relationship would have been like, had I been granted one.
I am always grateful for Inheriting her shoulders Poise and grace.

Cherish relationships, memories, and thoughts you have for someone, and not feelings from another who may have lived in a different chapter of their story.

Suzanne Smith (Dickson) my stepmother; through it all tried her best, loved the way she knew how, continues to be a piece of my past, present and future. Although we did not have the strong mother daughter relationship all girls yearn for, I've slowly learned we will continue to grow from a slimmer of hope, which has always kept the sometimes silent and unseen bond strong. I will always love the person I know she is deep within.

5 Generations:
Grandmother Dorothy, Dad, Me,
My Son Daryl, and Granddaughter Kamryn
as of date 7/28/2020 we are all alive although sadly never been together as 5, while some have not seen each other or spoke with in many years. Unanswered questions, so much confusion, misunderstandings, along with so many stories of the past which have never been pieced together. The child in me still wonders, as the adult cannot comprehend the generational sadness which tries to keep ahold

To my cousins who came a generation or more after me, be grateful you were spared A LOT, while NEVER judging the actions or lack of from those of us who came before you…

Kathy – Dad – and Myself

2011 Dad Visits For The Holidays – Always the Coolest

2018 was the last time spent with my father and younger sister Whitley together (my sons memorial weekend) also pictured is my twin Kathy.

We all have those people who were once in our lives for a short period or just a mere thought of existence because we were told of them, shown pictures, as we dreamed of knowing them, their voice characteristics, voice, anything that you could possibly relate to, as you continued to learn just who you are. I will forever ponder how life would or could have been, had I been granted a true moment with you all, so long ago...

"My Paternal Family"
Above:
Grandmother Dorothy (Dads mother)

Middle: Great Grandfather Herbert & Great Grandmother Dorothy Heinze (Grandmother Dorothy's parents)

Bottom: Grandfather Coleridge John Dickson Sr. (Dad's Father)

The only picture with myself, my twin and all our children together (my 3 and her 5)

The only picture of us with Dad (Me, Andrew "Mit", Kathy) 1993

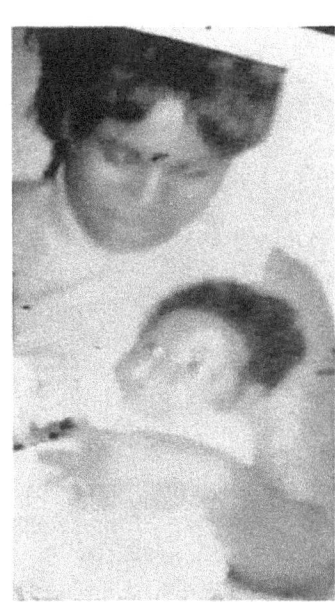
The only picture I have with my Mom 1969

Take pictures, for they will continue the story later on...

Pamela   Whitley   Jaquan

We may not share the same mother but, a bond that can not be broken, although you came along as I started having my own children you will always be my baby sisters and brother.
Pamela Pena, Whitley Gray and Jaquan Dickson.
I love you little ducklings….

Nephews & Nieces

Kathy: Davon (Lamar), Darrin, Jordan, Donjai, Dashon
Lisa: James (Lonnie), Dean, Theodore (Theo), Giraud
Andrew (Mit): Andrew (Duke), Nastascia

You all hold a special place within my Heart, the precious younger babies of Pamela, Jaquan & Whitley as well as my greats and future greats, Auntie adores you just the same. Keep pushing and doing everything, while remembering you are a true gift!

MY STRENGTH

Graduation! Daryl (CHS) 2006, Eddie (EVHS) 2010, Douglas (EVHS) 2012, You Did It!!!

Our Children Have Been And Will Always Be Raised As One... Hers are Mine and Mine Are Hers!
Karen & Kathy

Jordan, Dashon, Davon (Lamar), Donjai, Darrin

They say when you are an identical twins that your children are not only nephews and nieces, but in fact half siblings. We did not need science to tell us that our bond would be so close.
Forever & Always ~ Auntie Love You All So Much!

Antionette *Natasha* *Latoya*

Because of you I have my grand blessings – love you!

So, who are those people who fall in love at first sight and live happily ever after? What was and is love, and who was love? I remember being told during middle school and high school what I thought I wanted to hear and, oh, how we want to hear it all from someone who we thought was the cutest. Yes, I was one of those too. I had to link up with someone because something must be wrong with you if you did not have a boyfriend. To my surprise, everyone does not want to date for the reasons you do, nor do we even know the reasons why ourselves. To me any type of relationship had to be better than what I had endured at home. Anything had to be better than going straight home after school. On some days, the comfort of others' homes became what I strove for as I sought good attention from the adults, communication, and at certain times positive discipline. After several immature relationships on both parts (well, because we were immature kids), I smile inwardly as I think about what I considered my first true relationship. Ahhh, I just knew I was in love, and you could not tell me it was not going to be like the people in the movies that always had the perfect ending.

It was probably the summer after the eleventh grade, I knew this person as we previously attended grade school, middle school, and now high school. Interestingly enough, I think I fell head over heels with the idea that he came from a home I found so much comfort in, where the parents were still married and actually talked to each other; there was a little brother who bothered everyone and a sister who had to know everything going on, with everyone. I remember being at the home all the time. If you gave me a pen and paper today, I could draw the entire layout out, from the soft brown couch with the plastic covering it, a bunk bed in my boyfriend's room, and the kitchen telephone which hung next to the back door. The layout of the house was exactly as my own, although what happened inside the walls were so different.

Now let us dive into this relationship which I just knew was the greatest, well, I had to because anything was better than the unhealthy life I was in, the abuse I endured (but did not know was abuse at the time), and the weird boyfriend-girlfriend friendships I thought I was in prior. This time I thought for sure I was with someone who wanted me around for the right reasons, someone whom I could laugh with, watch movies with, and would walk me home and made sure I was all right when I got home. I frequently thought how things would have been or his thoughts if I shared what had happened with me inside my house years earlier. Would that have made our young relationship stronger? Hmm, after much thought in my mind, I feared it would not have and might cause one to run away, so as always, I kept the darkness deep within. Remembering some laughs and the night he was walking me home, it was later than normal, and I did hate leaving his house when dark because of this one house that had two Doberman dogs (some of you reading this know exactly what house I am talking about) who were never tied up and, of course, no fence. As we walked past this house, we heard the dogs and all I remember him saying to me was "RUN!" and that is exactly what I did straight up the hill as he threw rocks at the dogs. When he turned around and saw how far I had run, he could only laugh. You only have to tell me once to run! Finally, the feeling of protection by someone and comfort and safety sank in when he held me. Let us remember I was now 15 ½, and for the first time in my short hurtful life felt a hint of what normalcy was supposed to be. Smile for real if only for the moment and, most of all, breathe. Being young minded I started telling myself this will be my husband and wrote it on notebooks, doing what all giddy girls did and practiced writing what my last name would be and ironically planned my whole wedding as I sat in Ms. Undella's English class one day in 11th grade. I was going to be a princess and have everything pink in the wedding and then live as happy as I deserved to be. I find it amazing that many of us thought and think this way, teach this way, and continue to try and live with such hopes and dreams while having big imaginations about relationships. We have to start living in every moment while allowing each moment to be just that, the moment! So let me break down how different my mind and his reality were. Amazingly everything was genuinely nice with no hiccups the entire first summer, but how many of you know situations and people change when school starts back in session, ugh.

Titles and labels change, and competition creeps around. Yes, let us keep it real and call it like it was and still is for many. My wanting to believe I struck gold and the hurt of this thing called life had passed, quickly faded away as the familiar picture of my messed-up life started to present itself once more. I remember once while I sat in a home economics class, a girl (we will not name) showed up at the door, and as she peeked through the window, she caught my attention while holding her fist up to show me brass knuckles. I was kind of shocked at first while saying to myself, "is she serious?" I could not imagine why she was upset with me, but as I thought deeper while paying no attention in class, it came to me that she must have been there because of him!

How often do we allow the him(s) in our lives to cause more chaos, that we overshadow with our feelings of hope and want because of our needs? If one, then that's one too many. Immediately after class, I found him at his locker to inform him what had occurred and that it had better not happen again. Seeming surprised also, he said he would handle her. Hmmm, did he? I always assumed he did, and it was not until right now as I type about it, being older and a pinch wiser, that I say to myself, "man, how naïve were you?" while wondering what he really said to her, or if he told her the same as he told me. Several times after, I would see her walk past my street slowly ensuring that I saw her headed in the direction of his house. Now remember this was 1985, when we stayed outside more than inside while hanging out in the yard or on our front porches. Still holding on to what I presumed to be my first love, I continued allowing him over to my house at times and I would be at his, but not as much as in the beginning.

Once over at his house, I remember his beautiful outspoken mother telling us one day "you two better not come to me and tell me anyone is pregnant." We laughed because of course that would not happen to us. Fast forward to what she spoke came to light. End of high school year, 1986, day of senior skip day evening, he shows up back at my house and the rest made history and a significant impact in my life as a blessing was to come. The sometime relationship was not by my choice but was accepted, as more downfalls and hurt lingered. One highlight that bothered me for a long time and even after it was all said and done was the fact that he did not go to our prom with me while stating "it's not my kind of thing," but a year later took someone else to theirs and had the audacity to take pictures as well. Ugh and sadly I can still close my eyes and see them in the picture he in a black tux and her a blue dress, ugh wish I never saw the picture that somehow, I cannot forget. Wow, the things we allow in our midst and minds when we don't know who we are or what we're worth. When we think back over our life and truly reflect and finally be honest with ourselves, that is when we realize how we pushed our own worth and importance to the side, just to be with another while wanting to believe all would go reflect what the mind felt was perfect, or perhaps turn dreams into reality while seeing deep down we were never the priority, need or true want during certain times

Let us revisit my allowing him in my house on the evening of senior skip day, one month shy of graduating high school with hopes of going far away from this never-ending dark hole of a life and attend college in Norfolk, Virginia. Significant Impact = I became pregnant. This was when my hopes and dreams of a fairytale relationship along with one day attending college far away took a deeper detour down a painful road I was too familiar with. Well, the time had come now pregnant, and trying to hold any sense of it all togetherness while having to deal with the childish nonsense of, it all, not only by the person I knew was the father, but others as well. Still children in a sense, but now Having to grow up more than ever before. The rumors of "it's not his," "how does she know he is the father when he has been with someone else?" (his little prom girl) continued to be spiral throughout my pregnancy.

Fact: He was with someone else, not me! If I can share some insight with a high school student: Focus on your education! Date yourself, save yourself! Join in on as many school activities that you can, read a book, write a book! If you are the outgoing one, take no part in the drama, but in fact take drama class! Become lass president, debate a worthy cause! Get a part-time job, create a job! Laugh & have fun! Be and do, so much more…

Periodically, I would question if I was the only one amused by the comments spoken about me. Clearly, he knew the truth also, so I really did not care. My saving grace was I no longer attended high school, and when the pregnancy began to show I was now in community college. Believe me, no one cares about you there, especially if they don't know you. I did wonder when people who did know me and of my status would back up and reflect on themselves and stop focusing on people they were not with 24 hours of each day. I can only laugh a little at this because for the most part we were so young and all basically going through the motions of what was thought right at that time, as well as learned and ignorant behavior. My actions also in many fashions were merely a result of learned behavior, lack of consistent positive influences and direction, while no structure or balance was exhibited. Breathe and remind self of the child within who sought a way out while remembering to take one breath at a time and keep going no matter what. I was always wondering how, why, or when life would get easy. Did I deserve to have calmness and joyous moments like others? Or was it all just an illusion? What was I to believe when life seemed to be so unbelievable? The only thing during this time that brought comfort was the feelings I now felt from deep within, from the little being growing inside of me. A different unexplainable warmness was felt as I thought of loving this child as I have longed to be loved and if I had to struggle some and do it all alone, it would be worth every second as it could not be any harder than what I had to endure already in my short life thus far. Lonely months passed as I thought, "okay I got this," tired and getting super big I kept pushing. I remember sitting in my college classes very tired but refusing to give up because I had to get a little further than where I currently was, and I had to make my baby proud of me.

To my surprise, I learned I was carrying a baby boy! I was shocked because in my mind I thought I was surely having a girl as I already wrote the plan down years before: one child — a girl, a cocker spaniel dog, a Canon camera, and a Cutlass Ciera car, I thought was all I needed in life. Big dreams back then seemed more like an afterschool TV show. Surely, I am not alone with having had such unrealistic dreams and thoughts, and if you relate to any of this, I hope you, too, see growth within that has prevailed after finding your worth and self. Should you currently be someone seeking to learn more about yourself, always remember you are not far from being who you are meant to be! Stay strong and full of faith while keeping grace and mercy (our best friends) closer than ever. Remembrance will present itself as you learn more each day of who you really were created to be. Ahhh, you are so important and hold so much greatness!

With each day that passed, I fell deeper in love with my son who was on his way, I thought of many names to call him, and even though I had not seen his father for some time, I also loved the idea of having a Jr. to continue his family name. A part of me thought should I do that, maybe my son would act more like those people instead of mine who have hurt me so much. Around month six of pregnancy, here came the knock on the door, my baby's father stood on the front porch wearing a weird smile, with his best friend, while holding a crib for the baby. I should have said, "thank you" to his best friend back then for talking some sense into him. He was always the mature one between them. Thank You, R. I did question the father, "why are you here? I thought the baby was not yours!" as I opened the door, allowing them inside. I was sad and mad about our situation, but not crazy, bring that crib on in and, yes, set it up, too.

Over the next few months, we did the on again-off again relationship thing, but slowly faded apart as he did his own thing, which involved yet another relationship.

The time had come, and I received the best Valentines gift I could have ever received! My beautiful baby arrived on February 14, 1987, after 36 hours of labor, which included Friday the 13th and I had profoundly stated I will not have my baby on a Friday the 13th as if I could have really dictated that! Thank you, Lord, for answering prayers that I did not know I was sending up. I now know you had it all planned and already knew the day and hour my precious son would be born. I am thankful for his father who provided what was needed even when we were not together. I will add being more present physically while he was growing up would have earned him a gold star.

Parents, Be Present! The children may not have a calendar hanging up but do carry one within that is named "Emotional, Mental & Physical Needs," and they are marking the days, acting out or holding so much pain within when these needs are not met. On another note: Don't be the cause of hurt; be the reason they smile brighter; be understanding, caring, and loving especially when you don't feel like it; love more when they upset you, and more when you get upset because you had a bad day, which they had nothing to do with (get yourself some help in this area, for the child is not to carry your issues). Be the hope and joy they need and seek through you and love them more each day while remembering the first time you met them.

I am forever grateful and blessed for my son's grandparents, the Poole's, and the entire family whom I adore and will forever hold close to my heart. They have always treated me like family while making sure my precious little one wanted for nothing, as they continue to do so now for our grand blessings today. Things may not have turned out the way I wrote them down in my notebook while in English class some time ago, but when I look at my precious gift I smile and always whisper, "for you I would do it all over again." How interesting is life when we sit quiet for a moment and reflect on the good and bad of it all, a deep learning period for self. While sifting through the mind trying to make any sense of it all with the many "Why Did I" presenting themselves. Well, my school years were just as strange as some of the silly relationships I had prior to the one that made me a mom. I thank God for his tremendous mercy held over me as some predicaments I placed myself in and this could have made this chapter read quite differently. For when we do not know better, we will not do better! Please, please, please grab a hold of your children! Show them love, reiterate self-worth and YOU make sure to respect them first, before they seek what is yet understood in someone who is only focused on self-gain.

Writing these words, I think deeper about my childhood, had anyone ever looked at me to say, "You are so important, great, beautiful within, and going to do wonderful things in life." I was not fortunate to have a memory as such, although I now smile looking out the window while writing and thinking of my father who several times told me how proud he was of me. Hearing those words from Daddy was tremendous, wanted, and needed even if as an adult. My father's eyes, which are my eyes, show an abundance of love as it will always push through the hurt and sadness we have learned through generations to suppress deep within. Gentle tears flow as I can hear my uncle Dwayne's voice who tells me every time we speak now, "I have always known you were special, smart and would do good things, I am so proud of you and love you so much." Having a few other aunts and uncles who state something similar to the adult Karen allows me to feel warm within and a hint of what my childhood could have been. I will always carry so much love for those who have seen Karen, while loving her the way she needed to be loved. *Tomorrow is not promised; be a light for someone today.* Why must we date and not be alone for extended periods of time? Is it what we know because of what we were taught or not?

While working part time at a JCPenney jewelry repair shop in the mall during 1988, I met a guy who would come by several times a month to drop off and pick up items from each store. We would talk while he waited for his items to be gathered, and he smiled a lot as he told many stories of his dreams and how he planned to achieve them. He was a little older than I was and unlike me and unlike anyone I had ever been around. We truly came from different worlds with backgrounds that could never compare. Dating began this year, followed by marriage on June 8, of 1991, which is when his actions and demeanor changed (or was it always present and I was blinded), just in time for me to yet again endure another relationship that dissolved, but this time in a shocking, hurtful manner during 1996. Sharing this part of my life is primarily for more of my healing process to take place as closure continues to make its circle, and always designed to be a teachable moment for those who are preparing to enter a relationship, trying to figure out how to get out of an unhealthy one or needing reassurance that leaving was the best thing for you. There will always be a few bright moments in relationships, although we cannot let them overshadow how we are feeling mentally, emotionally, physically, and spiritually. It is not until we understand what these words mean for us as an individual that we can grasp a hold of what's actually happening with us at any given time.

Mentally —1: in the mind, 2: with regard to the mind or its capacity
Emotionally —1: of or relating to emotion
Physically —1: in a physical manner; 2: in respect to the body
Spiritually —1: of, relating to, consisting of, or affecting the spirit

Why did I rush into a relationship after being blessed with the gift that made me feel complete? The gift I could look at on any given day no matter how I was feeling and smile as my son looked back at me with so much assurance that I would always protect, love, and keep smiling back at him. Why did I go forward after my son's father came back one evening before I said, "yes," and married to see if I truly had moved on? Why did I watch him walk away down the dark street and let the other stay? Could it have been because I was still looking for something different, looking for the relationship that ended with the picket fence, a provider, and what I though was love, or was it because I had yet to know my worth and what I deserved, and not just desired? Me, one who joined the club who married for the wrong reasons, thinking the grass was greener on the other side, escaping a past I wanted to forget while praying it would not repeat itself, believing the stories and sweet talk, while wondering, "Did someone really love me?" mainly because of becoming pregnant once again. Once I did feel an abundance of love from him, during the time we endured a miscarriage. This happened the year before being blessed with my second gift, our son Eddie III who was born on June 18, 1991. He entered the world in a rush and was just what was needed as his shine and personality, so beautiful. I say children because my third blessing Douglas with the perfect 'lil face, never much for words and so huggable arrived on August 31, 1994. He was a pleasant surprise! Sometime beforehand with unclear dates in my mind I recall becoming pregnant before my last child, although coached into not following through with the pregnancy as I was told it was too soon to have another and my mother-in-law would not approve along with more talks. This rattled my mind, and today I wish I could go backward and follow my heart and talk to her as I am sure she may have had a comment but loved any and all children. My mind was rattled as so much confusion set in my 23- or 24-year-old mind. I kept thinking, "But we are married so what would be the problem?"

Sadly, I did not argue the case, nor knew how to then. Never remembering the date but can never forget the place, which was so cold along with him being so happy and content as if nothing major took place, was very eerie to me as I think deeply today reminding myself to breathe. So strange because my ex-husband was gentle and kind to his children. Loved to feed, give baths, played his guitar for them, among other things. Guess I cannot take away his love and what he tried to accomplish with them when they were children, nor will I elaborate much on what the children felt was lacking as they became adults as that's their story. But I will say support and unconditional love did not last long; fast forward later in life as judgment and hurtful actions came toward my son, his namesake, as his father and those associated with him did not approve of his lifestyle choices. Shame on them! I will never forget the hurt I had to undo while thanking God I was given enough strength within to do so. When my children hurt, I hurt so much more. I am forever grateful for their late grandmother Grace who was just that—"Graceful"—in all things: the love she poured on us, lessons taught, and teaching me to plant and grow collards and other vegetables, making the best potato salad while always having a small bowl minus the onions on the side for me. Today I am blessed with Sis. Connie Herndon at church who does the same, and yes, it is so good. Oh, and I could never forget my mother-in-law's sweet potato pie recipe, which I proudly use today with a little tweaking, pieces of her will forever be staples of our lives.

Amazing how we can neglect to see some of the puzzle pieces that God places in our lives that at some time or another keep us together, if only for a moment and without which we may not have survived. My marriage was nothing like I imagined it would be. I should have guessed it would not be as it was nothing like I once dreamed of as a child while entering with no understanding of what marriage fully entailed. Witnessing a tread of unhealthy relationships during my 22 years of life was eye opening and my inner self changed drastically when I said "I do" at Blank & Blank Justice of Peace Attorney's Office for which he paid $50. (That, too, should have been a sign if any, Blank & Blank.) I wore a blue and white sundress and flat shoes, and said "I do" just 10 days before my 'lil Eddie was born with about three or four people present. Sadly, I can only remember one of his aunts present as I try to place in my mind who else was there. The day was hot or maybe not as hot as I thought since I was ready to deliver a baby. Everything seemed so rushed, even as I think of it today. I always have moments that I wish I could have told my 22-year-old self to pull back if only for a moment to ask the many questions I have learned to ask today. I will always wonder if I had asked the questions, would I have closed some doors to other forms of abuse that I was not accustomed to. Sadly, along with emotional and sexual, the domestic abuse found its place in line, and no matter how used to any abuse you may think you are, you are not. The voice I lost so long ago was now suppressed even deeper within the girl who once remembered to breathe had to learn how to take another breath, if only for a moment. I am tired. "Not in the mood," "NO"—all ignored. Having no strength within to pull away or could I… and just did not know how to. How was I supposed to feel while wanting to refrain from arguments of any kind?

Assumptions and accusations continued while hopes of sleeping peacefully was always just a thought. Trying to take care of children when I could not take care of myself, extremely hard! Working at a school and other places while ignoring the pain and my feelings proved even harder. Emotionally I was broken and drained by it all. My grandmother once made a comment before my last child was born how surprised she was that I had become pregnant again as she knew how unhappy I was. I never expressed that to her; I guess just her intuition told her. Thinking about that conversation today, had she made the statement to me a little nicer with some love, I may have opened up about it and felt finally I can talk about it. No ma'am, I thought, we not having this conversation today with that "I don't know why you married him anyway" look she had on her face. Something within me knew all things must be happening for a reason, what was unknown and incomprehensible at the time. Trying to hold on while believing new babies, bubbles, and balloons could overshadow the emptiness I felt inside, I kept trying because that is what we were programmed to do when kids are involved. I am unable to remember exact dates or find my journals written during this brief period of time that still at times hold a great length of pain that will never be forgotten. After my last son was born, I looked at his face for a long time while at the hospital and said, "Wow, he looks just like my brother" (Mit), which I kept repeating. I do not think his dad cared for this as he never thought highly of my family, while carrying jealous tendencies.

Sadly, I lost my brother less than four months after I saw his face in my precious baby's face. I always question if seeing my brother in my son was one of the many signs I still receive today before I lose someone dear to me. This loss added more pain to an already broken relationship which I knew was no more as we only lived together but were so far apart. One evening after my brother's funeral I did not want to be bothered and because of my wanting to be alone and not touched I was yelled at, "I don't know why you don't want to be with me – I'm not the one who shot your brother!" Whew, what a blow to the gut, as my brother was gone as a result of suicide by gunshot. Instantly, I wondered did he even realize what he just said, why he said it, or how could he be so cruel to even part his lips to say it. Needless to say, I sought therapy because I thought I was going to lose whatever sanity I had left should one more uncontrollable act was to happen in my life.

Thankfully, I was able to find a wonderful counselor who stated I did cry a lot, but it was okay as it was helping me through the pain of it all. If she only knew the early layers I was also carrying while trying to cope with the shock of the new ones being added. After seeing her alone for some time she invited him into a session. The continued lack of accountability showed up to the session while staying oblivious to the hurt caused by his actions and hurtful words kept my thoughts in a "yes" phase. Yes, it's time to move out phase and as quick as possible as I didn't know what or who I was now dealing with and more fear crept inside. The shocked and disbelief he showed while in the doctor's presence as I shared the hurt and pain, I felt because of him was astounding and I had not even made it to the physical abuse yet. Halfway through the session I realized it was useless, and I needed to start a plan to move out and soon. Before the session was over I needed to remind him of what he said about my brother and how I was still hurting and felt that day. Unsure if an apology was given with the blank look that covered his face as I did not seek one any longer. I just needed to get my statement out and to hear myself say it aloud to him, so I could gain some inner strength from myself, confirmation I was done as I took a deep breath.

My words from that day forward became easier to say as the chapter of our failed marriage has ended.

I was no longer attracted to a man I realized I did not know and who did not know me.

I did not care that I heard he was with another woman and always at her home when we would not see him for days or weeks at a time.

I did not care to sleep in the same bed, so I eventually moved into the boys' room where we all slept on a full-size bed together.

I did not care that I would no longer have to explain where the change from a $5 bill was, or where I spent it.

I did not care that I would no longer have to worry about explaining why I looked at a house, car, or person as we drove down a street, no more having to say I do not know who lives there, the car or him.

I did not care that I finally shared my hurt at the cost of embarrassment to myself or toward the one who caused it.

I did not care that I ended a relationship so that I could reintroduce me to myself.

I did not care that I ventured onto harder times to raise my children alone, and would do it all over again 1,000 times.

As months passed and before I could leave, I kept my feelings to myself and limited if any conversations with him whenever he would come to the house, while I planned to move out. I befriended a genuinely nice man who I did spend time with once outside of the common place we met, although never in love nor wanted to be in a relationship with, just a 25-year-old seeking someone who seemed to care, spoke nicely, too, and said what I thought I needed to hear, but now that I relive it in my mind, was he really caring or merely taking advantage of a lost already hurt and confused young soul. Reflecting back, I am remiss to bring this part of the story up. Let me introduce my then husband's cousin's wife; yes, read it slow to understand. Well, I mistakenly confided in her during what I thought was much needed private girl talk and shared information about the man friend not knowing she was merely gathering information and could not wait to report it all verbatim. I wonder how she felt after learning how I had been treated, how our relationship was over and what was hidden behind our pretty closed doors or how she at that very moment placed my life in danger so her little self could feel big about reporting to someone who had already broken the marriage so long ago. I am still amazed as I write and still find comfort that I cannot remember her name, but will never forget the day she hung up with me only to rush and call him. Shortly after my conversation with her I left the house to attend an evening church service with his mother. (He stayed with the children.) While I sat in the choir stand preparing to sing, I began to feel the worst feeling in the pit of my stomach and knew at that very moment something was happening. I started thinking as the conversation I had earlier with the cousin's wife continued to play over and over in my mind as I instantly remembered not only her questions, but how she asked them. Immediately some fear came upon me as I started to wonder just how long this night would last after I returned home, and just how detrimental his actions would become mentally or physically. Upon being dropped off I could see him in the doorway, I said good night to his mother, she drove off and he waved to her, I think, and proceeded to lock the door as she drove out of sight. Yes, I was locked out by a man who I was basically a roommate with, a man who spent more time with another woman than with his wife and children, a man whose mother told me she spoke with the other woman and told her to leave him alone because he has a wife and children! (I told her no worries as she could have him.) Yes, a man who did not care that I was out in the streets in the dark after 10:00 p.m., having to walk extremely far to the nearest payphone, in a dress with shoes on, then back the same distance to the house. After a couple of hours, I was let back in but not before having to call his mother so she could make him open the door. This happened just in time for me to be taunted into the early morning. Had my children not been inside the house during all of this I would have kept walking that night and never looked back.

After everything that had previously happened with this man, this was the first time hatred grew deep within my soul for this person.
I do care that I will never be in another place with a man who will lock me out.
I do care that I will always have my own and give it to myself.
I do care that I can ask myself for $5 (hmmm, maybe that is why I save them).
I do care that I will no longer be dragged down the stairs or blocked in corners until someone finished a sentence.
I do care that I will no longer have holes punched in walls near my head or be called a witch in place of b**tch.
I do care that one day I called the police and moved out.
I do care that I no longer have to put on massive amounts of lipstick because that is what he liked, or that I have not used it since leaving.

I do care that I will never argue or fight over a man: he can leave, or I will.
I do care about my feelings.
I do care I no longer have to provide mental, emotional, and physical receipts, which drains from so deep within.
I do care about my children's feelings more, and more, and more.
I do care that I found some hope.
I do care that I met who I am supposed to be, "ME," even if I do not like me yet.
I do know now, praying helped, even when I did not understand.
"If ye abide in me, and my words abide in you, ye shall ask what ye will, and it shall be done unto you." John 15:7 (KJV)

During a period of hopelessness and despair, the strength that was suppressed and forgotten for so long ago presented itself once again as if to say, "Hold your head up; you are not finished yet." Planning a way to leave a situation that I never could have imagined being in lifted so much weight off my chest. Could I now continue learning about me and mine, could I stop acting like this family or that family, with my voice, could I have, be, and stay in my right mind, and not feel confused, could I?

Saving what I could and moving in with my grandmother and Rob for about two months before I could finalize plans to move to another state (where my father had previously moved) was scary but so necessary. But first the final day with him, which was sometime during the spring of 1996. Being unable to cope, endure, or explain why some of the arguments and fights continued and at random times caused me to call the police because once again the scene was not pretty within. "911, what's your emergency?" I quickly hung up. Dispatch returned the call, questioned who I was and if everything was all right; after stating I was fine and being asked if I was sure, the call ceased. I was thinking this call may have calmed the mood in the house. NOT a chance, as I quickly made the call again because by this time I refused to be pushed around again, have walls punched near my head and continue being called names that did not appear on my birth certificate. "911, what's your emergency?" I quickly and firmly stated "Please send an officer because one of us is going to die today and it won't be me," after that response, several police cars promptly arrived, as the officers entered the home they were greeted with two different stories of what occurred. My story was allowed first as I shared with so much fear that all I wanted to do was leave the home without hearing his condescending and manipulative voice. Then his side of the story was told while stating something as such, "I don't know why she is so upset or acting so hysterical." Truly the Dr. Jekyll and Mr. Hyde cards were being played right out in front of me on this day clearer than ever before. The look on the officer's face was like "yeah, right" as they waited for me to pack and leave safely. I quickly packed three small black duffle bags and left with my children, with some peace and what little dignity I had left.

A couple of weeks later when I returned with a U-Haul truck to gather our belongings, I showed up with two of my cousins who stood watch as I felt I needed to be cautious. Of course, he stated, "You didn't have to bring them here." My thoughts were "You're lucky they don't know the full reason I am leaving." The things we victims did/do while protecting the abusers is truly astounding. Upon reaching the door, I was only allowed to look through the crack of the door as he was in control of what I could and could not take. I was given a table and six chairs that I had previously purchased, the full-size mattress and box spring my children and I had been sleeping on, along with whatever else he packed. I wouldn't know fully what I had until I reached my next destination and looked in the few boxes he gave me. I later learned some of my children's memorabilia, photos, trophies, and who knows what else was not passed through the door and would never be touched or seen by myself or the children again. Talk about the need to have control, pretty disgusting that this had to happen to me and continues with so many others. Knowing what I now know, I'm glad I didn't try and return for other items that were eventually replaced just to have to endure further humiliation and being controlled, which may have proved detrimental to my mindset as I was about to move so far away.

Feeling good within myself, I whispered to myself while walking away from the front door, "Let the rest go because one day you will have better, along with peace of mind." After driving off that day, so many layers of hurt and pain began to fall off of me even though the days ahead were so unclear. Ironically while stopping at a grocery store close to the house later on the same day so I could stock up on goodies for a long car ride ahead, lo and behold who do I see through the store window smiling while pushing a shopping cart like a happy child with one foot on back coasting about, as he talked to others around? Yes, him. "Ugh," I thought, "wow! I'm so glad he's so happy to be free," as I drove off to another store so as not to run into him. Then shortly after, I met up with my older son's father who took our son for the summer months while I relocated and got settled in. He also gave me extra money for my travels, a hug, and reminded me to contact him if anything else was needed. Leaving all I knew behind, I started the six-hour journey from Connecticut to Virginia with two of my three sons. Traveling alone with one who had just recently turned 5 and another shy of 2 years old was a bit scary, but this needed move along with my adrenaline rush made for a safe trip. Note: The ex did try and say, after learning my oldest was staying, that I could have left the younger two with him as well so I could set up a home faster. No thank you, as you will never say I crossed state lines and abandoned my children. Trust = Gone! Life was so different after moving to Virginia, a true shock as I think, "Wow, we live Down South now!" Some say you been here for so long now it's home. Unless you've ever had to relocate with trauma in your baggage you will never understand the unsettling feeling that lingers on when your change had to occur because of a situation and not by choice, making it hard to call any place "home."

Time passed after the boys and I moved. I even allowed them to travel back and forth over the years when they got a little older, and two children experienced a year of school back home also. I believe a year or so after we moved was when we returned home for a Thanksgiving holiday or should I say returned to Connecticut as I haven't had a family home since 1987. During this holiday, the children and I went back by train, visited family and the boys at their family homes, then my ex offered to drive us back to VA so we wouldn't have to take the train. I accepted the ride, and it wasn't long before he stated maybe we could work out better as a couple in Virginia. Hmmm, let me think about the couple of days of fake happiness together before you returned back to Connecticut, while also remembering how I was once locked out of the home, forced to leave with what I was allowed to take that was passed through the crack of a front door, having to work two jobs, no support, got a raggedy apartment, made sure my children ate every day even if it meant I didn't so they could have more or leftovers on the next day. Yeah, I don't think so! Have a safe trip back to your home.

Life, one thing I did not choose but instead was granted learning to pay close attention to something even if I don't fully comprehend while being stuck somewhere in between trying to figure it out and which road to take why and when while always breathing Hardships, hurt, and pain continued to prevail during my short lived life although I would relive it all again and so much more for without I would not have been in the position to have been blessed with my three gifts, for without I do not know where or how I would have ended up as I carried such a load of little or none, that always proved rewarding in its own way.

Pay attention to negative signs and the red flags that are present, especially when you're giving, doing more, and being more for someone who does not reciprocate. Sadly, the cycle is hard to get out of and very easy to fall back into, especially when a person knows you're in a vulnerable state. Think about actions first and words second, but always while reminding yourself just how strong you actually are, no matter what. Then repeat as you continue to remind yourself each day.

I came up with some questions while previously working with a person who walked along the path I once journeyed, as well as those losing self for other reasons. Should you not be able to answer them quickly while having a calm feeling within, please think about your relationship, your situation, and yourself.
What's your favorite color?
What was your favorite color as a child?
Is it the same as now?
Do you like baths or showers? Why?
What's your middle name? If you don't have one, do you wish you did and what would it be?
Favorite movie?
Favorite book?
Rainy days or sunshine?
If you could do anything at this very moment, what would it be?
Do you ever relax while quietly listening to music while picking out each instrument, then comparing with what you're wanting or needing to do for you, mimic the instruments and play your notes in your mind while doing all you need to do for yourself?
Are you completing the puzzle of your life before trying to help someone else with the corners of theirs?
Are you allowing yourself to learn who and why you are?
Also ask yourself questions relevant to you, as they can/will keep you above water when you feel yourself drowning because of someone's actions toward you.

Self-esteem: confidence in one's own worth or abilities; self-respect.

Confidence: the feeling or belief that one can rely on someone or something: firm trust.

Worth: sufficiently good, important, or interesting to justify a specified action; deserving to be treats or regarded in the way specified.

Love: a feeling of strong or constant affection, a great interest and pleasure in something.

Domestic violence (also named **domestic abuse** or **family violence**) is violence or other abuse in a domestic setting, such as in marriage or cohabitation. *Domestic violence* is often used as a synonym for *intimate partner violence*, which is committed by a spouse or partner in an intimate relationship against the other spouse or partner, and can take place in heterosexual or same-sex relationships, or between former spouses or partners. In its broadest sense, domestic violence also involves violence against children, teenagers, parents, or the elderly. It takes a number of forms, including physical, verbal, emotional, economic, religious, reproductive, and sexual abuse, which can range from subtle, coercive forms to marital rape and to violent physical abuse such as choking and beating.

Sexual Assault refers to sexual contact or behavior that occurs without explicit consent of the victim. Some forms of sexual assault include attempted rape. Fondling or unwanted sexual touching. Forcing a victim to perform sexual acts, such as oral sex or penetrating the perpetrator's body.

National 24/7 Hotlines I would be remiss to share as I think about how much different my life would have been if I knew of one safe number to call, while I remembered to at least breathe through it all even as a child.

Domestic Violence 1(800) 799 -7233, 1(800) 787-3224 (TTY) ncadv.org

Sexual Assault 1(800) 656 - HOPE (4673) https://rainn.org

LGBTQ National Hotline 1(888) 843-4564 https://www.glbthotline.org/national-hotline.html

National Suicide Hotline 1(800) 273 -8255 https://suicidepreventionlifeline.org/

National Runaway Safeline 1(800) 786-2929 1800runaway.org

Human Trafficking 1(888) 373-7888 (TTY 711) Text: 233733 humantraffickinghotline.org

Stay true to you
Say what you want
Sincerely mean it
Stop pulling back
Stay focused
See what's ahead
Study the past
Seek truth
Share hope
Survive!

Sadly, my present and future seemed to hold more pain as the cycle of dating or thinking I was dating the persona of whom I thought I wanted to be with proved just as painful emotionally and mentally in several more instances. So, who deserves true happiness, what exactly was a healthy relationship and how in the world do I date, be in a relationship, understand anything fully after all of this? What is normal, what is real, what is truth, just what is it all without any pain attached to it? Twenty-seven years young I sat dismally contemplating it all, remembering many times as a child when I would pull myself out of the picture of my life while gazing from outside, slowly taking one breath at a time before blinking and moving forward to what was to happen next while praying for anything better than what was. How I wished wise people were near, television shows exhibited true life, people around paid attention to other's emotions and true needs, and so much more. This way I could have been taught self-love and so much more without having to wait for the realization that it was already tucked deep within. I'm still amazed how it all works, the person who loves and cares for others much more than self, continues to seek just a pinch of it back in return. Knowing now that we all have the gift of discernment (the ability to judge well, perception in the absence of judgment with a view to obtaining spiritual guidance and understanding) but we allow the pain of circumstance, situations, and people to block this gift at any given moment. Dating after marriage or what I assumed to be dating relit the green light of pain with no red or yellow blinking anywhere in sight for some time. I always wondered how people stayed married for long periods of time. Are they truly happy as they celebrate their silver or gold wedding anniversaries? Are the smiles and hugs real and did the people who celebrated with them honestly believe the present they gave would be used, or would the party end and couples retreat back to their corners? Was it all as blissful and joyous as the party? I think so much more than I have ever in my life, amazing how we can now reflect on periods of our life which during the times of occurrences we thought that was what life was all about! As I think about relationships after my divorce, a large part of me is incredibly sad as I think over what happened or not. Why did I feel as if I wasn't enough after always giving everything, I had to offer? Many times, we as women nurture, provide and set the pace for others to be comfortable, accepted and wanted, but it doesn't come back to us in the same package, lack of respect, and never acknowledged with a simple "thank you" for trying to be or being so awesome. As I write these words and feel a slight headache trying to push through with just the remembrance of it all, I start to feel some warmth and a little comfort from within take over as I tell myself I'm only bringing up these thoughts to share, help and encourage another so we can begin focusing and paying more attention to ourselves and not waste our needed energy on others who don't even know our likes or dislikes. I will stop reliving, thinking less of self, and especially blaming ME for what was never meant to be. The end of this chapter will also end any thoughts of how I could have changed or been different or did more for this or that person, as I know wholeheartedly, I have always given and was always the best me. Releasing internal hurt from failed relationships (which were failed from the start) truly enhances your inner worth as you're reminded just how important and special you are. Becoming the person I am today I realize my worth was and still is so much more than any relationship that actually carried no titles. When I say "no title," you may wonder what I mean. Well, think about how we want to be labeled, introduced, and mentioned as all that we think means so much and makes us who we are, while more than fewer of the entire relationship or lack of is so superficial. Here are a few titles I speak of, words that, sadly, dictate to many how we should or should not treat someone, while feelings, emotions, and respect at times never show up. Girlfriend – Boyfriend – Partner - Babe – Honey – Sweetheart - Significant Other – Other Half – Lover – Sugar – Hubby – Wifey – and the other mushy cute nicknames. Yes, I'm His - Yes, I'm Hers - Etc. Etc. Etc. labels that may not be spoken or recognized between both parties within the so-called relationship, and surely more times than fewer never spoken or exhibited by one of, especially in front of their peers. Thinking more about this subject, I clearly see how the ones we least expect to accept, appreciate, and be honest with us while currently in our so-called relationship are the ones we continue to walk around and ignore. Surely something must be wrong with them because no one is that nice, trusting, honest, or would ever want such a mess like me. Oh, the outer may look appealing but are they equipped for what's lingering within. Time doesn't stop, pause, or take breaks. What it does while ticking forward and never backward is show us when we should open our eyes fully to who has always been in plain sight and reachable, while in many ways already providing comfort within the mind and spirit while never focusing on the physical. Ahhh, what "God Sent" must mean. I have to giggle at myself sometimes to keep from crying while in disbelief when I think of the times I allowed myself to ignore or dismiss others' behavior toward me while obviously being disrespected. Lack of knowledge, stripped innocence, dangerous learned behavior, along with the absence of positive influential strong people for one to witness, learn, and grow from, is one of our biggest hindrances.

Oh, to be young and do it all over again, would I then be who I was meant to be? Honestly, I believe not. While hitting each letter on the keyboard my loud tap, tap, tap becomes softer as I slowly stop, pause to look out the window at a tree preparing to bloom. Take a deep breath, count slowly from ten to one and remind self to keep pushing as more memories start to cause a frozen effect from deep within. Continue whispering to self, keep going. Remembering several individuals whom I somewhat dated between a seven-year period after moving to Virginia. So much can be shared although a lady never kisses and tells in writing. The faces, voices, cologne scents, demeanor, and time spent together at times is as clear as a few moments ago, within my mind. Who were these men? To me they each represented pieces of a puzzle that was yet to come together, as all the pieces were never within just one of them. So, who stood out holding some of the pieces to a puzzle that never seemed to come together? With a deep sigh, I think of the Handsome one, the Suave one, and the Gentleman, as with all relationships good and bad lessons are learned. After it was all said and done, they and I continue to hold a high level of respect toward each other. Rare but true!

Oh, the Handsome one, who captured my every thought from the first time he passed by a hug that warmed my heart and a sense of protection whenever around. I thought this had to be love as everything was so different from what I had once known and his gentleness overshadowed everything I had once known or experienced in a relationship. This one took my heart in many directions as I effortlessly gave with hopes he would take control and lead the relationship in the direction I felt it could go. Lack of communication was a hindrance but as I longed for him to want only me, if only for a moment proved overwhelming. These hopes held us together for a season while forever was never an option. The hurt, pain, and butterflies continued to linger as the on again-off again relationship swayed about until I could no longer hold onto what was not meant for me and just me alone. No longer would I cry in disbelief, wonder where or why, while fighting a battle that was lost long before the fight even started. They say you get one true love in a lifetime, but is it really true love if one person commits more than the other while giving their whole self? I believe he held a hint of something tucked deep within for me, especially after receiving a letter one day which was full of everything I needed to read, hear, and know long before he had written it, such a time as this. Deep thoughts and butterflies followed for a time as I was reminded of some good days, while hurt jumped in gently whispering thoughts of other days.

Mr. Suave, so well put together, charismatic, with the unforgettable scent and strong embrace, the one who liked to get dressed up and fine dine the night away. Gentle and serious at the same time, with a heart to help all. I cared for him although wouldn't allow myself to fall too deep because I knew our inside relationship would never make it outside. Meaning = girlfriend to some but not to all. I sensed at times he didn't think I was enough for him because he knew the me at the moment, the woman in survival mode, raising three children and working wherever at the time while figuring out the new life I was thrust into. Trying to remember if we ever discussed what I aspired to do or had done previously. I wonder if he knew I was a teacher, grew up with a father who enjoyed music, and shared our culture through theater and arts so much that it trickled down onto me. That I did ballet, tap, and jazz along with so much more that was tucked within the madness of my younger years. That I held so much passion deep within to do everything I could imagine and much more or did he just see a mother of three who was a waitress for the time or holding down other meaningless jobs to make ends meet after fleeing a really bad situation causing me to live in places far from what my children and I were accustomed to back at home, with trips to Cape Cod Massachusetts and so much more in between the madness of it all. Conversations as such were foreign for me to share and not a strength of mine back then, as I sought others to take the lead or at least place the end pieces of the puzzle called relationship together. The reflection of "what if?" of my past proved larger than the relationships that apparently were not to be.

The Cool nice one, from day one after being introduced by a mutual friend, smiled with truth and honesty while being a comedian at heart with his no rhythm self. The time had come in my life where I was able to finally smile without having to do so through pain, doubt, or for show. Being able to laugh with someone was a rarity, was the piece to the puzzle finally starting to come together, was this happiness. He did live up to the title and because of him I learned the meaning of friendship with someone of the opposite sex. I used to think distance and our schedules were the cause of us not going further in the relationship, but in time I learned the Lord had different plans as we remained friends from afar. Time had passed when I received the call informing me that he was getting married. A little surprised but happy, I wished him many blessings while my mind replayed the movie "Brown Sugar" and we were the main characters (somewhat funny but ironically all relationships can compare to a movie or in fact be a movie). Long after this news,

I couldn't watch that movie and to make matters worse my silly friend who I call "little sis" happened to be in the car with me during the call and after I hung up, looked at my face, laughed a little and said, "You're not going to cry, are you?" Shanica, YES, you're a "Jerk" but I love you, our sisterhood, and your tremendous support still to this day. Could I find another who uplifted, supported emotionally and spiritually, one so close to the pieces of my extremely tough puzzle of life, and who loved my children just as I did his? Ahhh, the Cool one, "my Jordan — his Pippen," I thank you always for the continual respect, happiness, honesty, laughs, and true friendship after it all, and sometime later during a phone call yelling at me to get off the phone and prepare myself to get married!

How does one find self or gather oneself together enough to prepare for a healthy relationship after enduring and making it through so much and at 35 years of age? Is it even worth the time and energy anymore? I think "wow!" as I know people who at 30 years old are just starting to deal with the small pieces of what I have written books about from as far back as six years old. First, seek knowledge of what it is you are trying to enhance, regain, repair, exhibit, or take part within. This in addition with so much more will either start forming a strong foundation or start the process of filling in the cracks of a broken one.

Self (noun):
a: (1): an individual's typical character or behavior
   (2): an individual's temporary behavior or character
b: a person in prime condition

John 17:5 And now, O Father, glorify thou me with thine own self with the glory which I had with thee before the world was. (KJV)

Healthy (adjective): d: (1) prosperous, flourishing

Jeremiah 33:6 Behold, I will bring it health and cure, and I will cure them, and will reveal unto them the abundance of peace and truth. (KJV)

Relationship (noun):
a: the state of being related or interrelated
b: the relation connecting or binding participants in a relationship: such as
   (1): kinship

    (2): a specific instance or type of kinship
c: (1): state of affairs existing between those having relations or dealings
    (2): a romantic or passionate attachment

Colossians 3:14 Beyond all these things put on love, which is the perfect bond of unity. (NASB 1995)

Once upon a time, they lived happily ever after. Never once have I read a fairytale that didn't include sadness, fear, happiness, and love all wrapped up in the storyline. Do we think they are written as such for many to pay little or no attention to, or merely for an exciting storyline and later a movie? I, being the hopeless romantic my entire life, grew up believing something had to be better than what actually was, while finally understanding that my past suffering and failed relationships were not in vain, but merely training tools for what was to arrive next. So was it finally (f-i-n-a-l-l-y in my exhausted voice) time for the little girl who remembered to breathe to gain some peace, for the young lady who always tried to exhibit a touch of grace even when not knowing it to now have a pinch of it cast upon her, and would the young mother who through it all tried, tried, and tried again as she sought a little mercy for not trying more, while using a sound mind when she possibly could have done better?

Scripture states "Whoso findeth a wife findeth a good thing, and obtaineth favour of the Lord." Proverbs 18:22 (KJV). Would I ever be the wife who was considered the good thing? Could I be the one who was the reason someone obtained favour in the Lord. Was this possible after all and everything I had been through, was I even classified in the Lords eyes as a good thing anymore. Would the wedding I once dreamt of and wrote down in the eleventh grade ever come to light, would the girl who fantasized of looking like a princess in a beautiful white gown ever walk down the aisle while not settling and actually marry the man who adored her more than she ever thought she deserved, and did she, I still believe in fairytales. The year was now 2004 and I remember being so tired of it all, unlike ever before: the so-called dating and tired energy that came with it all. This truly couldn't be what life was about. I had to be worth so much more than what I was receiving or accepting. What did the little girl who finally remembered to take "One Breath at a Time" deserve, and did she have anything left within her to keep pulling herself out of dead end relationships, was this her season to break free and finally meet a person, any person, the person who was meant just for her?

Sometime during this year, my children left Virginia and headed back north for a few weeks, as they have some summers before. This was the time; I would try and work extra hours, redo their bedrooms with new bedding and stock up the home with goodies before they returned to be prepared for the upcoming school year and try to regroup a little within myself. Something was very different this year as my mind continued to roam while the need to pray crept in like never before. I remember watching a lady minister or evangelist on television who was preaching, but not just delivering a word but sharing her testimony as well. Her testimony from a time years before was so profound and hit so close to my home during this time. Quickly realizing her message was meant for me to hear at that very moment, I began to think and receive the whole message unlike any other message I had heard before. Weeks passed and maybe a few months, those words, the message of Dr. Juanita Bynum (author of *No More Sheets*) continued to repeat itself loudly in my thoughts as I vaguely remember praying to be released from the bondage of a painful past, current relationships, or lack of, and finally be able to allow healing to enter in while understanding fully who I was. I no longer wanted to be who I thought I was supposed to be, the one who dated for comfort while trying to fill a void or other reasons that would cause more pain within, some way or another. Always knowing something was supposed to be different in my life, that there was someone we called God who I wanted to believe remembered me just as I wanted me to remember him.

Having been born Baptist with my beautiful mother who sang in her little church choir, then after losing her, attending my stepmother's Episcopal church as a child followed by an AME church with my first mother-in-law, then moving and entering a non-denominational church, then eventually going back to Baptist, with unknown thoughts of the future happenings proved very confusing for someone who was just trying to believe in something. I continued to pray as I sought a little purpose, if only for a moment. Yes, I questioned was I praying right, was I asking or saying what needed to be said? I didn't know! I just knew it was something I needed to continue doing more than less. Being someone who attended church on and off, sang in choirs, just doing "Church" deep down during those times really meant nothing. It wasn't until I finally allowed a breakthrough to happen that I then realized that church was what I was doing on the outside while nothing was happening within me on the inside. The realization of the Holy Spirit hit hard one night as I became very restless. My children were still in Connecticut, no friends were over, and I just sat in the living room and started thinking, which turned into prayer as I kept thinking about "No More Sheets" while remembering I was capable of letting hurt and dead-end relations go. I was just as strong on the inside as I was on the outer. After some time, I ended up in the middle of the living room floor, weeping, while whispering a prayer. Will I ever know what I said way back then? Absolutely not, but I always remember that moment during the year of 2001, in a little house, on a little street called Aspen, in a little town named Culpeper, in the state of Virginia, after many hours of trying to get up but being forced back down as the time of being saved was yet complete, as strength needed to continue being poured within, as the little girl and now the woman needed yet another hug from above, while comfort and peace took over like never before. I didn't know what I was experiencing or why it was happening until it was complete, until being released after 4 or 5 hours of weeping, praying, and being poured into, until the pressure of life or what I had known of it was lifted, until I knew I was given control of me.

My Lord was all I could think as I thought about my children, then led to remember the kindness within and about one man. Which takes me back between the years of 1999 through 2004, a period when I met the kindest man with the gentlest demeanor. I thought, "Wow. I've known him for some time," but I actually didn't know him at all. I would see him periodically when I would go to the store where he worked. We would talk about items I may have been shopping for while he helped me find things. Somethings I knew where they were, but I enjoyed his company, so I would let him walk with me to show me anyway. More than less our conversations got longer while whatever relationships issues I may have had had at the time became the topic as he listened with kindness and a gentle smile. I never thought of us as anything more than friends. Surely, he was too nice for me, and I didn't think I was deserving after all I had been through, with him seeming to be someone who had been through absolutely nothing in comparison and such a sweet person. Of course, I always was kept in mind that there is no such thing as true love especially since all I had to talk about was failed relationships and all the problems within. I would wonder at times how or why he was being so nice to me, was so soft spoken, gentle, caring, showed love for his family, honored and happy to be a deacon at his church, and doing all of this so effortlessly at the same time. Little did I know, he was keeping mental notes of everything I said, what I liked in the store and life in general, or that he was paying extra attention when I talked about my children while appreciating my love for them that much more. I surely never imagined that he was praying for me, and praying harder after I shared my dating dilemmas with him, for I don't think anyone has ever prayed for me in this capacity, and I never until long after that he always told himself from the moment he laid eyes on me that one day I would be his wife. Time would pass as we continued to speak in passing at the store throughout this five-year-period and no matter who I was with, I would smile and speak to him as he did me. Some asked, "Who's that? Why do you talk to him? He's not even your type, what do you see in him?" etc. etc. etc. Sadly, I listened to them at times while thinking, "Yeah, he's not my type, but what's the harm in having someone nice to talk to every once in a while?" My goodness, had I looked at the big picture of it all back then, I would have come to the realization that my so-called "type" apparently was not MY TYPE at all, as no relationship had worked or was working anyway. As time moved along, eventually during one of our conversations, to my surprise, the gentleman asked me out on a date, I'm sure to his surprise I surprised him when I said, "Yes." Well, to be honest, I surprised myself as well. The date was planned: dinner and a movie it was! I did ask a girlfriend to come along with her friend so we could make it a double date as a part of me didn't want to go alone. Would we have something to talk about the entire evening? What if it got really awkward? What if he wasn't the same person outside of the store? And the thoughts continued. We decided to ride together on the date; this would possibly make communication a lot better and less awkward. I don't know why I felt the need for this as our conversations were always nice, but those were held at the store. Part of me still felt he was a little awkward because surely no one could be this nice while always keeping in the back of my mind, after prayers and all that there had to be a catch. Once the date was planned, Monica and I joked around saying to each other that he better not have a church suit on when he walks outside for the date. She and others continued to question my interest in this man, and my statement more or less was "Well, he's nice." Date night arrived, and since we all lived in the same apartment complex at this time, it was easy to meet up. Pulling up to his building, we anxiously awaited him to come outside and — whew — no suit! Although he did have on khakis and a button-down shirt, we chuckled in relief as he walked (I am sure) nervously to the truck. Off to dinner and the movies we went, us in one cinema to see Deep

Blue Sea with L.L. Cool J and them in another. Prior to the movie we went to dinner where he spoke maybe a sentence or two. I am sure it was awkward for him as it was his first date ever and I did drag along company.

Time passed after the date, and we continued talking when ran into each other at the store or on the phone sometimes. He also invited me to a few church services which he took part in, and soon became a minister, which was surprising. Actually, the only times I would hear him speak with a projected voice was when he preached a sermon. Through it all he stayed true to his self, his faith, and was always such a gentleman. This was very foreign to me because nice, pure, honest acknowledgment, while showing so much positivity and attention toward me, was something I just could not get used to. So, me being me, my mind drifted toward the thought that something must be wrong with him, amazing how we never think something maybe wrong with ourselves. As time went on, I continued confiding in him regarding one relationship or another as he always patiently listened while providing a little hope within. Periodically, he would send me flowers while always having the right thing to say, until I started feeling a bit overwhelmed while allowing his kindness to resonate in my mind as creepy because no one could be like the fairytales I once dreamt about, and relationships I was in and out of were the opposite and what I thought I needed.

What was I to do with someone who treated me like a princess, while the flesh was used to the ways of the world? Oh, as I close my eyes and think never had I been courted so, listened to, respected on such a level or given so much attention. The gentleman once made me a mixed cassette tape with all his favorite R&B jams on it, surprised me with a dinner with some of my favorite foods, and one Christmas invited me over so I could find a tree with gifts tucked beneath, of everything from the store I ever stated I liked or admired as we walked about. His listening was impeccable as he always awaited my next word. I could not shake why his kindness started making me feel uneasy as each day passed, and sadly, one day I had my friend Vicky call him to ask that he stop sending me flowers and back off a little. He did just that for a moment until one day he sent flower seeds instead with a note stating something like, "You asked me to stop sending flowers, so I'm sending these seeds that maybe we can plant together one day." I started to ignore him as time went on because I only thought of him as a friend but he seemed to want more, which I could not nor thought I wanted to give him. Being in and out of relationships and having thoughts arising from past trauma and never seeing a positive relationship nor being in one that amounted to anything caused me to fear the good in the gentleman. Childhood Trauma = Trust issues and little hope. Surely, in my mind I kept thoughts that there was no such thing as a true gentleman since all I could remember for so long was how I was hurt so much more than ever loved by men, starting with the innocence of my childhood which had been drastically stripped away. Even after my profound prayer I continued to think, "How could this man be any different from what I was accustomed to and not assault my intelligence, mind, body, and soul like so many others. Well, time had passed and now I'm in the season which led up to me being tossed and turned into that serious prayer session during 2004, which I spoke of earlier. "My goodness, just what exactly was all this praying about?" I thought. What was God revealing to me and what exactly was I saying or feeling within myself? My God are you serious? Why was I led to think about the one I called the Gentleman and in the same breath I kept whispering he's a little weird, too quiet and definitely not my type. God, I know I must be getting on your nerves by now, truly I'm so sorry and promise to get it together! Yes, I couldn't get him out of my mind and surprisingly I began to anticipate the gentle thoughts of past conversations and the pure kindness that was always present. I began feeling bad by the way I had treated this man as I kind of started ignoring him and at one time had my girlfriend Vicky answer that phone call to ask him to back off a little. After much thought about my negative actions that came about, partly because I listened to comments made by others and still thought, "He's just too nice for someone like me." Eventually I decided why not send him a letter with one of my poems attached as a form of apology? "Would he respond or even care anymore?" was all I could think about after the large envelope was dropped in the mailbox.

Do You Ever Wonder

Do you ever Wonder why you were dealt the cards you had to play
Do you ever Wonder why your bed you had to lie in was made that way
Do you ever Wonder why you can't sleep at night when you are so very tired
Do you ever Wonder when the road is going to finally straighten up and stop going around & up and down
Do you ever Wonder why God takes the Strongest people first And at the Weakest times in your Life
Do you ever Wonder why people always want more from you than they would ever give you
Do you ever Wonder when the Battle is going to end
Do you ever Wonder why things can't stay the same when everything is calm
Do you ever Wonder how God Graces you with a smile when you're crying deep within
Do you ever Wonder how you can make it so far on so little
Do you ever Wonder how people can't say I DO and really mean it
Do you ever Wonder how you are still Holding on when the rope seems to be getting shorter & shorter
Do you ever Wonder why relationships can't stay in the mushy stage
Do you ever Wonder why such a small word like L.O.V.E. has such a powerful meaning And why so many people never knew the meaning...
Do you ever Wonder why it takes more muscles to frown than it takes to smile And Wonder if people knew that, why would they continue to frown
Do you ever wonder how Negative words can break you down, but you can get right up from a Punch!
Do you ever Wonder why the grass isn't Greener on the other side
Do you ever Wonder if this is how it is Always going to be
Do you ever just Wonder I Always Do...

I believe it was less than two weeks when I received a response via mail. It truly felt like a month as I kept telling myself, "I'm sure he's mad and will never forgive me while having moved on." As I reflect now, I think, "Man, we both must have been so nervous, because we could have driven across town and either hand delivered the letters or just talked." Anyway, the notes are precious and will always be stamped deep within. I began to read his reply while feeling unlike ever before, as I whispered each sentence while my eyes moved slowly down the page, I started to understand the meaning of grace and humbleness, and to my surprise he understood why my actions took place the way they had, that I was in fact trying to pull away from others and that it had nothing to do with or against him. As I continued reading, my heart softened as he proceeded to apologize for seeming impatient while knowing of my relationship/non-relationship happenings. He was also grateful for the time he had to reflect and enhance his relationship with God as he no longer was a deacon in his church but in fact was now a minister. Still a little intrigued by this letter, I thought, "Wow, I prayed for a praying man, never once thinking I would be sent a minister!" After finishing this beautiful letter that seemed to be written for a fairytale and surely not me, I noticed a poem was attached that was shockingly a reply to the poem I sent him. I kept thinking, "Is he serious? Is he this nice?" and "My goodness, there is such a thing as a gentleman."

The Gentleman's Reply

I Wonder

If you still have that bright smile
If you still like rainy nights
If you still like walks in the park
If you still laugh the same cute laugh
If your hand is still looking for another to hold
I Wonder
Why I can preach in front of hundreds, but still get a lump in my throat around you
Why I still get butterflies in my stomach when you come near
Why I still think of you now and then
Why you still affect me like no one else ever has
I Wonder
What if our beginning was just the first chapter and not the whole book
What if God has something more in store for us
What if the perfection you saw was meant for you
What if we had really tried Yes, Sometimes I Wonder

Garry M. Brown   2004

"Oh, my!" I thought as emotions ran deep within. He really wondered and most of all cared about the one he called "sunshine" from day one, the one he said would be his wife since the first time he laid eyes on me, the one he saw as a princess and one day his queen. Obviously, feelings were mutual at this time, and we were supposed to be together forever. Within several months, the Gentleman, Mr. Garry McArthur Brown, such a humble, quiet, kind, and caring man sealed the deal with a proper proposal. Since I kept a card in my wallet that listed my ring of choice (a girl needed to be prepared), it made it a pinch easier for him when that time came. Since I have three sons and always need to feel them in all things, my engagement ring consists of three diamonds and is still as beautiful as my three gems. Proposal Day! I would have preferred him to be a little more romantic and surely not at my job in the parking lot. Oh, but grateful am I to reflect on Tuesday, November 16, 2004. That day a shy man with a little faith and a big heart got up enough nerve to once again ask if I would spend the rest of my life with him, but this time with the ring while softly playing "This Very Moment" by KC & JoJo playing from his car. I can close my eyes and play the day out in my mind as I sat at my desk wondering, "Who in the world is in the parking lot with that music on?" Before the doorbell rang, I would have never guessed him. Full speed ahead to engagement and family photos while planning a wedding for May 14, 2005. I wanted a fall wedding as I love everything about that season, but he won with an earlier month. Him being the one who always paid attention to calendars was focused on lining up the date around the same time his rental lease was up at the apartment he shared with a couple of his siblings. I agreed as long as it could be on the fourteenth, which used to be my favorite number for several reasons, since May had the fourteenth on a Saturday, that worked. The wedding full of many people and so much love was planned and turned out wonderfully as I finally got to wear a princess gown and walk down the aisle to a man I had cried for, prayed for, and was blessed with long before I had even known. As with all weddings there are some hiccups, including ours: My father couldn't make it to walk me down the aisle but praise God, my oldest son did while my younger two looked just as handsome as junior groomsmen. We lost the 80's music we chose to play for an hour during the receptions, only to find it later in the back seat of the car as we arrived at the Poconos for our honeymoon. The arch at the end of the aisle wasn't completed with flowers and garland added before I entered. Someone was fired. I can laugh today but then, come on people! My grandmother arrived late, so she missed the opportunity of lighting the candles. I didn't get to have the color pink, which is my favorite color and written into my childhood wedding dreams, as I also have the nickname of "Pinky." The story with that is interesting as choosing dresses was very interesting with the bridal party and after trying on many dresses, some ladies not showing up, etc., I let one person choose and didn't care any longer. Today I wish I would have slowed down as I now tell the brides I may work with when coordinating weddings. Okay breathe, I got that out now back to the fairytale that still melts my heart today while thinking back. Naturally no relationship is without flaws, but can I say how blessed I am to be with someone I have never argued or had cross words with? Finally, someone whom I fully related to, whom I could agree to disagree with and whom I enjoy so much peace with while not having to worry if something is not going right, not worry about arguing over the little things and surely not worry about whom he is with when I am not around. To be in a relationship that didn't present triggers from the past or create any for the future is gold. It took time for a complete relationship to enter my life and I shall no longer carry the wonders of it all anymore. Shall we dance in the rain as if no one is watching, ride off into the sunset, no longer have to kiss frogs to find my prince and could now hypothetically wake up from a dream? The fairytale that I never thought could be is not over, so with hesitation to share more of a beautiful chapter in my life while showing an abundance of happiness, I pull back. For the little girl in me doesn't want to "jinx" anything, as happiness in my puzzle of a past meant hurt and pain was to follow. The fear built into the little girl who grew up reminding herself to breathe through it all always saw people meeting goals, achieving the toughest tasks, start to be happy as life was finally making sense, pass away. While the adult in me does understand what God meant shall always be today, tomorrow, and forever more, for the Lord will never leave nor forsake, and I will not be left comfortless. As my wonderful husband and I do life, love, and ministry together, we are so grateful for the journey the Lord has entrusted to us as we fulfill it together. Wow, year 2022, new beginnings as we continue building from within, build our business, exit our second traditional Baptist church home and move forward in ministry led by the one above.

The Lord makes firm the steps of the one who delights in him; though he may stumble, he will not fail, for the Lord upholds him with his hand.

Psalm 37:23-24 (NIV)

It Was Always in You

"But by the grace of God I am what I am: and his grace which was bestowed upon me was not vain; but I labored more abundantly than they all: yet not I, but the grace of God which was with me." 1 Corinthians 15:10 (ASV)

Whoever said, "You can't do that — why bother trying?" "It's not possible," or just simply, "No!" had no idea just what mold we are made from. I remember growing up dreaming of being a school teacher, having a beautiful wedding and children one day. Would this happen to me since I did not see or have examples around. I don't even remember attending one wedding during the first quarter of my life. Oh, to dream as I doodled on paper during my 11th grade English class my big plans, the color wedding I would have, what my last name may be "giggles" only to sit here today realizing they all came true! Not necessarily in the order or last name planned, although I achieved the impossible and still shock myself daily as I believe in so much more. When we listen to our heart and flow with the feelings, we learn what is already within us. Our dreams are merely the map of what is to become our thoughts, a hint of the achievable, and saying yes to what we believe in, confirmation that it will happen. Listen, feel, dream and become what's in you!

5th Pastoral Anniversary Service March 2018
Pilgrim Baptist Church, Locust Grove VA

She not only fights to pull through her own battles She pushes, encourages many even as tears begin to flow She understands hurt, pain and some occasional joy She will continue to stand tall, for if one can see then it was surely meant to be.

My husband Garry Brown and myself Pictured far right second row (white dress shirt and tie, black shirt, and face mask). Photo by Kim Atkins

I painfully read George Floyds last words.
On the day of George's murder 5/25/20 cameras rolled with
paramedics on the scene, officers continue to hold him down,
9 minutes after the knee of one officer continued to keep his knee
On Floyd's neck he is heard saying "Man, I can't breathe", goes limp
while completely motionless and THEN he is loaded into the ambulance.
Photo by Kim Atkins 6/6/20

#SayTheirNames

I pray for a child who is scared of the police.   Continuing with George Floyds last words.

Growing up I remember the black and white pictures of protests, civil right leaders, and those who spoke up for justice.

Today our pictures may be colored, new leaders are stepping up, but the fight is still the same!   #justice

K.D. Brown

Photos by Kee Shepherd 6/6/20

We stand for everywhere
not just where we live,
We stand for equality
We peacefully stand in unity,
We lift our voices to be heard
not to yell at another
#WeAreTired
#BlackOutTuesday
June 02, 2020

K. D. Brown

Sharing my story while ministering and mentoring others with a little bit of grace and gentle prayers, continues to help me take "One Breath at a Time" while being reminded that I have so much more to give from so deep within. As I move forward in this journey called life and the puzzle pieces finally begin to align one with another, I exhale while thinking how amazing life is now. I can smile for real and love as I am loved and not only by with my children but as a whole with a husband as well. Happiness, ahhh, his is what it feels like. So, what's next for the little girl within who chuckled as she could now say I made it, healed and free from the torment of a dark past? I'm almost 50, and everyone is healthy and happy, so why not plan a birthday party over the next six months with my twin sister? Well, if we can get past the color choices and agree on something. Yes, we are doing it! Or were we, as reality began to sink in and just as I start to see the puzzle of life coming together tragedy knocks on the door, causing the little girl within to curl up once again as she gently whispers to herself "why me — again " and now my child.

My tallest sunflower has fallen as my heart now beats at a different pace. Sharing my story while ministering and mentoring to others with a little bit of grace and gentle prayers, helps me to take "One Breath at a Time" while being reminded that I have so much more to give from somewhere deep within.

Some will never know how hard it is to take a picture with two children and not three. Photo taken at my first book release and signing for "One Breath At A Time" March 23, 2019. Pictured with my oldest Daryl and my youngest Douglas, my precious middle son Eddie is on Daryl's shirt. Always with us, always in our hearts, we feel you...

Myself, Linda Mosley Johnson (my children's Godmother), Pastor Ferne Cannady Sapp, Kathy Dickson (my twin), God brought us together around the 4th grade while grace keeps the sisterhood together. Photo: August 25, 2018 after my Eddie's Celebration of Life Service.

"I thank my God every time I remember you.
in all my prayers for all of you, I always pray with joy
because of your partnership in the gospel
from the first day until now."

Philippians 1:3-5 (NIV)

Too many times after this grand loss, I literally gasp in constant disbelief. One of those who know of my life, the hardships, and continual endurances asked me, "Why do all the bad things continue to happen to the same people? Why does God allow such things?" Being in my cloudy mindset at that time, I surely couldn't answer since I could not understand at that moment, either. I gently passed the question to my husband because at that very moment I couldn't give my regular response, a generic response we mumble too frequently, that God makes no mistakes, everything happens for a reason, it is all making you stronger, or preparing you for what's to come next, etc., and because at that very second, I also cried internally for a different response. All that I gain strength to do will forever be done while holding onto every moment, Memory, and thought of my lil Eddie. His wisdom, passion to travel while so free, and love for so many shall continue to be found within my heart and all that I am. May the pieces of his entire existence forever overshadow me, his brothers, and all who knew, loved, and appreciated him. Always ESIII "EDDO." Always, We thank you for all the love We thank you for all the support We thank you for all the compassion We thank you for checking in on us Although, Please be mindful when you run into us We may smile when outside, but are crying deep within We may not be ready to talk about the site And surely may not want to know the exact location Also, please place your flowers elsewhere I know this is comforting for many But for myself and some others, causes triggers, hurt, fear, and tears As you keep uplifting our beloved We know you are also keeping us uplifted ESIII, lil Eddie, NuNu, EDDO, Eddoxxl, Eddie Spaghetti, Eddie Bauer, Black Yogi, my Precious, and so much more… We will remember them all while talking about you, keeping you so present, and continuing to love and adore you so much! Just as we did during our yesterdays.

Remembering to Breathe

I always wonder why the shortest words have the strongest meaning. Should we look up the definition of grief we learn it states that the word is a noun and explained as deep sorrow, especially that caused by someone's death. Never followed by a paragraph that tells you how to deal or cope, should you pray more or less, when will you be happy again, how to continue raising children, loving a spouse, moving on and on and on. I wondered all these things as shock sunk in: this couldn't be my life, were these cards truly dealt for me? was this the bed I was made to lie in and for how long? It's never easy thinking about grief, feeling it and most of all ever talking about it, especially when the reality of it all sinks in a little further day after day. My daily journey begins with reminding myself to breathe just one breath at a time, and more so when I remember my yesterdays. Having lost a mother and brother long ago, I surely thought the pain of such losses was over during my lifetime. How could I fathom or ever endure another as I thought this more times than less each day? Life seemed to finally be getting on the right path, I smiled as tears seldom fell while thinking, "I made it!" and "You did it!" Yes, it's time to plan a fiftieth birthday party and enjoy the next 50, since the past was a mere dream — or was it? Enjoying what I like to call "this thing called life" now turns down a darker street than I could ever imagine. Six months shy of turning fifty I can vividly remember early one morning the three loudest knocks I have ever heard, Pound, Pound, Pound. My heart started to pound just as loud as I kept reminding myself to breathe, until the moment I couldn't anymore as one officer began to speak of my 27-year-old son who had been involved in a tragic car accident. Having been two short years ago, which will always feel like this morning when the knocks landed on my doorstep, I know it continues to be God's grace that kept me then and so much now, His grace which reminds me to pause to make sure I am breathing when someone sadly says "I am so sorry," "Oh my God what happened to him?, "He this or He that," or simply give me the sympathetic look as they whisper, "I can't even imagine…." My reply to that is always, "I never want you to have to." Coping comes in many forms for me as I remember my son Eddie Servance III by honoring his legacy by doing all he loved to do through the ESIII Foundation I have established, baking sweet potato pies for our annual fundraiser, hiking with Eddie as we all wear tie dye attire each year on the day he walked to be with our Father, collecting silly and character socks during his birthday month to donate to those in need as he loved helping people, but his socks more. Oh, to see his face as all these actions continue to give not only me strength to carry on one more day, but also all who continue to look for his smile, sarcasm, and love. During these times, an overwhelming sadness may come and go more than other days, but this is when I embrace the rainy days that we love, seek out the red birds and blue butterflies and of course the tall sunflowers which he always captured through his photography ventures. I also pull more strength by looking at his two brothers' beautiful faces as I whisper, "I still have three...." Each day brings new strength and hope as I breathe away the fear and many thoughts of what's next. Doing thousand-piece puzzles, listening to music, writing, and reading assist in keeping my heart beating, especially when the beat matches the sounds of gentle rain drops. Upon my devotional time I couldn't help but be drawn to: Psalms 29:11 The Lord gives strength to his people; the Lord blesses his people with peace. (NIV) Jeremiah 29:11 "For I know the plans I have for you," declares the Lord, "plans to prosper you and not to harm you, plans to give you a hope and a future." (NIV) I thought, "Hmm, what's happening with the 29:11 theme?" as they are validating each other while knowing what we would endure during this thing I like to call life. How grateful am I for allowing God to introduce me to my two wonderful friends Grace (unmerited favor) and Mercy (compassion), whom I invite to stay with me each day while knowing for without whom I would have lost myself long ago. I ponder many of my son's wise sayings or the quotes he would reiterate such as Benjamin Franklin's "Lost Time Is Never Found" (again) as I finally realize the depth of his thinking and appreciation for each moment he was granted. For if we start living as if each moment truly meant something, while breathing through the happy and sad times with assurance that each second, minute, hour, or day was in fact "The Moment" then and only then can we enjoy what was, will be and is to come....

Good Morning Lord, We come to you on the day as we seek your presence and strength one more time. May you pour continued blessings upon us as we work tirelessly, scared and sometimes quietly. May you sprinkle grace and mercy on each of our heads not only when we enter familiar places but extra when we leave them. Father God, may you remind us of your why, when, or how and no one else, so as we listen and feel your presence we stay assured that you are always with us....   We love you Lord, Amen Surviving & Thriving

The Lord is my shepherd; I shall not want.
He maketh me to lie down in green pastures: he leadeth me beside the still waters.
He restoreth my soul: he leadeth me in the paths of righteousness for his name's sake.
Yea, though I walk through the valley of the shadow of death, I will fear no evil: for thou art with me; thy rod and thy staff they comfort me. Thou preparest a table before me in the presence of mine enemies: thou anointest my head with oil; my cup runneth over.
Surely goodness and mercy shall follow me all the days of my life: and I will dwell in the house of the Lord forever.   Psalm 23 KJV

Because of Them

Children are a heritage from the Lord, offspring a reward from him. Psalm 127:3 (NIV) Working hard for many years with the passion to always complete the next task continues to teach the ones coming behind me to keep stepping forward, embrace life, make it what it should be for them! The smiles, warmth and simplicity of this thing called life is so much more important than hoping someone remembers the accolades that we may have been earned by a person or place who forgets about you sooner than later. Oh, the joy in raising three sons, even when having to do so alone for a period. Watching them exhibit my nature and drive but most of all peace during the storms meant I did something right. Fast-forward to grandchildren: my goodness, double the pleasure as they love to mimic "Nona" as I teach them to make homemade sweet potato pie, fold laundry, sing, do skincare—we love Vaseline (can you tell I have girls so far?), most of all knowing how important and precious they are, like my babies who came before them. They say you overcompensate for what you didn't have growing up, for those coming behind you. I do in the form of making positive and loving traditions and memories while protecting them from the red flags I once fought through. Children do not bother us; they are merely interested in learning, growing, and being!

Train them up with grace and thanksgiving.

Heartfelt

For we walk by faith, not by sight. 2 Corinthians 5:7 (NKJV)

It's easy to forget our favorite color as a child or if we even have one as an adult, whether we like bubble baths or showers and, as we get older, possibly our own middle names — should these questions quickly be asked of us. How wonderful it is, that deep within we shall never forget the feelings of our heart, the yearning for something not only grand, but enough to make it through just one more day. Year after year, I not only wondered how I could continue doing for others, but also why I want to for so many when only a few reciprocated in the same fashion. Why help the less fortunate, when I could end up in the same boat, as times got hard, harder, and at times its hardest! Pondering this thought, I remember a time when Jesus was on a boat during a storm and at that very moment, I genuinely believed His words "when We get to the other side." My own boat called life, with many cracks and leaks I call losses, continues to make it to the other side. This is when I whisper, yes "*We*" while knowing in my heart the Lord, along with my greatest losses a Mother, Brother, and Son, will always guide me as I continue believing through the storms. The heart has four chambers, although able to beat with only one.

"I WILL MEDITATE ALSO OF ALL THY WORK, AND TALK OF THY DOINGS."
PSALMS 77:12 KJV

Raindrops and Sweet thoughts

"God is in the midst of her; she shall not be moved: God shall help her, and that right early." Psalms 46:5 (KJV)

As the rain gently falls, I continue grasping a hold of myself, listening to the tap, tap, tap on the Window, smiling while remembering I made it! No longer allowing yesterday to be my tomorrows, I frame memories of a mother taken too soon, leaving some of her pain which was later forced onto me. Daily I imagine hearing her voice while she sang in the choir at a small Baptist church on a tiny street corner, wondering, "Did she cry while singing songs of praise as I do today?" Ahh, I can only believe she did as her tears felt like raindrops, which caused sweet thoughts while her praise was lifted higher as peace made an entrance. Oh Lord, most precious Lord, today I come to thee with open arms asking you to touch all within my reach, those I know and not. Lord, grab a hold of the ones who are ever so lost deep within and continue to cause hurt and pain. Lord, step into the homes of those who are weeping at this very minute because they cannot understand why them. Dear Lord, continue to be a comforter day in and day out, while knowing you are appreciated, loved, and always welcomed. We give you glory, honor, and praise while awaiting answers only you can and will provide. Amen.

"ME" Day in and day out we wear many masks; daily I seek to understand the person behind all of them…The hurt, pain, joy of this thing I call life comes in many forms. To see your face in those coming behind you as you grow, heal, and breathe, One Breath at a Time during it all, is what Grace must feel like, what Hope concludes to, while Peace abounds close within.

Make faces And laugh Out loud – Especially When It Hurts

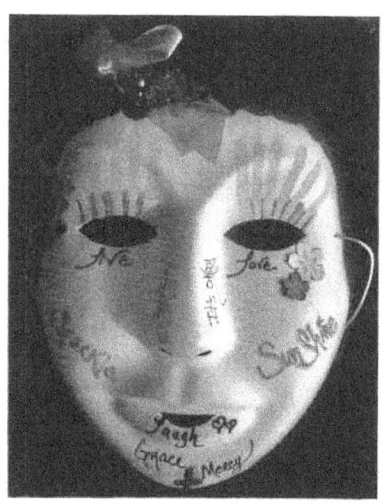
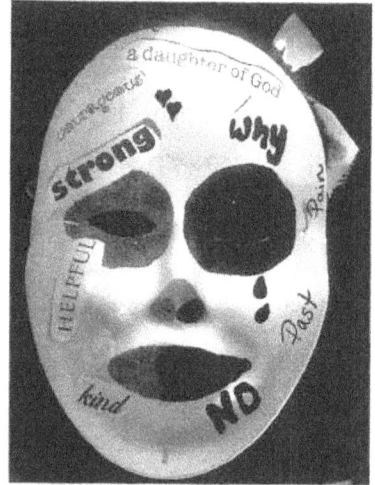

Daily We Wear Masks, Learning Who We Are Is The Key to Being The True You!

I created this mask with a group of ladies sometime around 2015-16, with a very compassionate and caring instructor (Sara BB). We had to make the outside of the mask (left picture) show how people see and perceive us, while making the inside (right picture) exhibit how we truly felt, what stayed in our hearts and mind as we carry so much within. Feeling strong one second, until the why(s) of the mind take over and so much pain prevails. Which is when we ask ourselves "Who Am I"
We sometimes change our masks periodically throughout the day, Who and Why is Karen…

Grateful /ˈgrātfəl/ adjective feeling or showing an appreciation of kindness; thankful.

I'm glad I can remember when I had so much less than I do now, but still able to share it all with my three, especially when it snowed inside or no funds to enjoy outside. And so blessed with an abundance of memories that I can remember. I'm glad I remember when playing solitaire, Jax, Spud, 4 squares, doing puzzles, and playing board games were the highlight of the day... and blessed I still enjoy doing some today. When family dinnertime meant something, while saying, "Thank you, Lord, for this food" and "now I lay me down to sleep" made us smile, as we believed in what we were saying so much. The Covid epidemic has reminded me to think more in some cases, be grateful for church within, the internet, cell phones, Netflix, and the occasional time to chill. All of which is so needed at their appropriate times. More than anything let's remember how precious time is, and what we would do with more of it, if granted!

time /tīm/ noun 1. the indefinite continued progress of existence and events in the past, present, and future regarded as a whole.

ONE DAY

One Day we might be old
One Day someone will sit and ask us 100 questions
One Day we will be gone
One Day someone might miss us
One Day someone will appreciate us
One Day someone will smile at what we used to do
One Day pictures will hang high as a little one looks at and wonder One Day understanding will come as memories flow
One Day your favorite flower will sit on someone's table, desk, or in a car
One Day others will watch your reactions, posture, and eyes
One Day Grace will answer as Mercy carries you toward the next step
One Day Jesus walked, talked, helped, healed, cried, was ignored, as people thought less of,
But kept loving and caring as instructed, since that is what He knew, believed, and is…
Oh, to believe and love abundantly, we too can today, tomorrow, and always!
One Day…Can Be…Today

She continues the fight through the struggles that arrived when she was born. Trials, tribulations, nor fear can hold her down. She was created for more than what she sees, what He has delivered her from and trained her for is unexplainable!
She will keep taking One Breath At A Time through this thing she calls life...

Learn each day that the obstacles placed along our path are merely shaping us into who the Lord has created us to be at this very moment, while training us for where we must go. It is then even at our weakest that His light will shines brighter amongst us, for if we would open our eyes to see, while allowing whom I call my best friends Grace and Mercy in, then some understanding may abound.

Stronger Than She Knew

The word of the Lord came to me, saying, "Before I formed you in the womb, I knew you, before you were born I set you apart; I appointed you as a prophet to the nations."   Jeremiah 1:4–5 (NIV)

Sometimes in the transition of it all, I began to express myself with less assertiveness. In my mind, I was reminded my thoughts, cares, and concerns would not be validated. Who would listen to someone who felt so broken, abused, and alone? I was sure my inner self was poking out for all to see as I continued to think judgment was taking place. Choosing distance as my comfort, I pulled back to observe, while keeping a complacent look on my face, I slowly learned I was someone. Hope arrived as I stretched my arms wide to uplift prayer using words I thought were fitting, while warm tears flowed ever so gently. Learning to look back in a different light while pulling strength from the hurt, joy from the hardness and love from the pain. The child with so much held within, Broke Out and became stronger than she ever knew she could while loving who she grew to be. I now see what was meant for me whether easy or hard I now see why it had to be, no more worries no more complaints no ifs, ands, or buts will I ever express because I now see what was meant for me…   Shall we prepare internally for what is to come externally so not to be affected emotionally, mentally but most of all spiritually by it all, once again.

Someone's Always Watching

"She opens her mouth with wisdom, and the teaching of kindness is on her tongue." Proverbs 31:26 (ESV)

Many years ago, as I waited patiently for the dentist to call my name, I continued writing notes after talking to the receptionist about my first book I had written. The conversation caught the attention of a child who was paying close attention, who then softly asked, "What's your book about?" As I began to tell her of it, to my surprise she looked at me with a familiar look I had seen in the mirror many times as she responded, "I have been through a lot too." I talked for a few more minutes so I could spread some comfort and hope before I was called to the back. The remainder of the day, I felt myself looking ahead at this child, then behind as I reflected on the words from the book *I Know Why the Caged Birds Sings* by my favorite author, the distinguished Dr. Maya Angelou. God knew I would read it! I gained insight as I was still healing from childhood trauma, but more direction being planted within, as I had become a vessel, unknowingly, who would carry tidbits to release when needed as I did when the encounter took place with this child. People will inquire why we do this or that while feeling compelled to ask more if they see our works, and gifts stem from another who may have paved the way, which then allows us to do the same. Think about someone's actions, words, or life that continue to aid you along the way today. Then release it with another whose path you will cross as you first notice that oh so familiar look.

During life, obstacles that are placed along our path to shape us into who the Lord is molding us to be —even when it hurts us, takes our smile away for a period, and we lack understanding — we still can see a light. Many months after being called to minister and now as I go through so much pain in my life, I have stopped saying, "not now and not me" while profoundly saying YES! my God, I will be obedient and minister your Word! On this day, we announced this information to our church and now I share it with you also. All Glory to God!

About The Author

Karen Dickson Brown has devoted her life to being compassionate and caring while spreading love and hope to those who cross her path. Mrs. Brown is a native of Stamford, Connecticut, the child of Mr. Coleridge J. Dickson II and the late Patricia E. Dickson. Mrs. Brown shared her parents with two sisters and one brother, and later in life was blessed with three younger siblings. Mrs. Brown, a former school teacher in Connecticut, continues to hold a special place within her heart for all children. Serving as a lifetime advocate for abandoned, misplaced children, and young adults has been very fulfilling. She has found joy in assisting pregnant girls who were alone and displaced, giving support during labor and delivery, but most of all unconditional love and a lot of hugs. The numerous persons who have crossed Mrs. Brown's path allowing her to mentor, assist with housing needs, and teach basic home and life skills has in return blessed her tremendously.

Mrs. Brown has worked in the mental health field for over 25 years, was the previous director at a DV/SA Agency, director of development at a homeless program, as well as providing case management and supportive services within allied agencies. Mrs. Brown received the Catalyst Purple Ribbon Award in 2015 from the Virginia Statewide Domestic Violence and Sexual Assault Action Alliance, which "honors one working specifically in the field of domestic violence for demonstrating exemplary commitment to restoring power and hope to victims who have experienced domestic violence through the provision of direct client services." She continues assisting those in need while thriving daily with the Lord's assistance to reach and touch all who have yet to find their voice as they silently cry out for help. Mrs. Brown founded the ESIII "No Limits" Mentoring and More Foundation after the loss of her middle Child, Eddie Servance III, a 501c3 nonprofit mentoring program providing support, love, and guidance, the EDDO (Educate, Decide, Develop, Overcome) way, while also catering to the needs of those suffering the loss of a child. Mrs. Brown, a licensed minister and certified life coach, has served within the Ministers Wives & Ministers Widows Association of the Wayland Blue Ridge Baptist Association, Virginia Chapter. Mrs. Brown is the previous first lady of Hopewell Baptist and Pilgrim Baptist Church, both of Virginia, where she enjoyed singing in the choir, serving as a deaconess, teaching Sunday school, and working within the women's ministry. Mrs. Brown, along with her husband, are grateful where the Lord is leading them as they strive to reach the multitude through their outreach efforts and online ministry as the Lord prepares them for their next assignment. She is married to the humble Pastor Garry M. Brown, mother of three sons Daryl, Eddie, and Douglas, and Nona to five precious granddaughters all of whom she adores as they keep a hint of joy and peace living within. Mrs. Brown, minister, mentor, motivator, certified life coach, author, and so much more, she lives daily by the Word with her favorite book in the Bible being Proverbs as she strives for more wisdom each day.

www.ingramcontent.com/pod-product-compliance
Lightning Source LLC
Chambersburg PA
CBHW080453170426
43196CB00016B/2788